Loving
Learning

ALSO BY KATHERINE ELLISON

Square Peg: My Story and What It Means for Raising Innovators, Visionaries, and Out-of-the-Box Thinkers

Buzz: A Year of Paying Attention

The Mommy Brain: How Motherhood Makes You Smarter

The New Economy of Nature: The Quest to Make Conservation Profitable

Imelda: Steel Butterfly of the Philippines

Loving Learning

How Progressive Education Can Save America's Schools

TOM LITTLE and KATHERINE ELLISON

FOREWORD BY AYELET WALDMAN

W. W. NORTON & COMPANY   New York London

For information about permission to reproduce selections from this book,
write to Permissions, W. W. Norton & Company, Inc.,
500 Fifth Avenue, New York, NY 10110

For information about special discounts for bulk purchases, please contact
W. W. Norton Special Sales at specialsales@wwnorton.com or 800-233-4830

Manufacturing by RR Donnelley-Harrisonburg
Book design by JAM Design
Production managers: Devon Zahn and Ruth Toda

ISBN 978-0-393-24616-2

W. W. Norton & Company, Inc.
500 Fifth Avenue, New York, N.Y. 10110
www.wwnorton.com

W. W. Norton & Company Ltd.
Castle House, 75/76 Wells Street, London W1T 3QT

1 2 3 4 5 6 7 8 9 0

Contents

Foreword

by Ayelet Waldman

One afternoon, while waiting for my youngest son to exhaust himself clambering up the face of a rock wall, I decided to count the number of schools with which I've been associated, both as a student and as a parent: fourteen. Fourteen schools that run the gamut of ideologies and philosophies. Progressive schools, traditional schools, religious schools. Public schools and private schools. And in all those many years and all those many institutions, I had not met anyone like Tom Little.

Tom understood children on a profound, intuitive level. Within a few weeks of enrolling our three younger children at Park Day School, we had a meeting with Tom in which he flabbergasted us with his insight into each of them. He *saw* them in the way no one had before. He saw how they learned, what means and methods best suited them. He saw their place in the group of children, how they communicated and participated. He knew just what he, their teachers, and we needed to do to make room for our children to experience *joyful learning.* In many ways, Tom Little saw our children more clearly than we did ourselves.

More than that, Tom took delight in our children. He was tickled pink by children—ours and everyone else's—genuinely fascinated by how they thought and felt, by what they said and did. And his delight was infectious. It reminded you why you wanted to be a parent in the first place. He would, even in the most anxiety-provoking of atmospheres, the dreaded parent-teacher meeting, crack one of his massive smiles at something a child had said or done, shake his shaggy head in rueful, appreciative admiration, and make you feel not only that everything was going to be just fine, but that your child was something precious and magical, a person with the capacity to do good in the world.

Doing good in the world meant everything to Tom. His fervor and relentless drive to make a difference were critical in forging a remarkable school, a place where learning is defined both by joy and by empathy. The book you are about to read shows that Tom's insight extended beyond the individual child to the project of education as a whole. His decades as not merely the head of Park Day School but its heart and soul gave him a perspective on the project of education that is critically important right now, in this period in which our society is in the throes of a terrible anxiety about education.

Last night I sat in a crowded theater with hundreds of Tom's friends and colleagues, the parents of children whose lives he shaped, and the children who were transformed by his insight and the joy with which he undertook the project of their education. This book proves that Tom was, as one speaker said, the preeminent voice of Progressive Education in this country. He was, as another pointed out, hopeful, relentless, and dedicated to the project of education and to children. But the thing that people said again and again was that Tom was profoundly gifted at *gratitude*. At Park Day there is a tradition that, at the close of every event or performance, whether it be a class play or simply a story read aloud, students give one another what they call

"Appreciations." They point out the elements in which they took pleasure, or which caused them to think more deeply or to see things in a new way. This foreword is an appreciation of Tom, an expression of my gratitude that he was a part of my life and the lives of my children, albeit for too brief a period, and that he had the strength—the *relentlessness*—to complete the task of finishing his book so that many others can benefit from his wisdom. But far more important, the work you hold in your hands is Tom Little's own "Appreciation." It is his Appreciation of children and of the magnificent project of educating them.

In this wonderful book, Tom Little shows us how to embrace our history and restore delight to the process of learning. Even as we grieve our loss, those of us who were blessed with his compassionate insights and joyful presence are thrilled that these will now be shared with the community at large.

Loving
Learning

Meet Me at Park Day

Park Day School poster created by
David Lance Goines.

To imposition from above is opposed expression and cultivation of individuality; to external discipline is opposed free activity; to learning from texts and teachers, learning through experience; to acquisition of isolated techniques by drill is opposed acquisition of them as means to attaining ends which make direct vital appeal; to preparation for a more or less remote future is opposed making the most of the opportunities of present life; to static aims and materials is opposed acquaintance with a changing world.

—JOHN DEWEY: *Experience and Education*, 1938

Come with me on a tour of Park Day School, where I've been privileged to work for the past thirty-eight years, first as a teacher and then as head of school. Throughout that time, our school, spreading over four shady acres in downtown Oakland, California, has been a nurturing oasis for curious, creative children, and a laboratory for smart solutions to the crises challenging American education.

Unless you've been on a long news fast, you already know that America's schools are in deep trouble. Desperately trying to squeeze in time to improve student performance on government-mandated, high-stakes tests, they've been cutting back on art, music, PE, and even recess and lunch. But all these tests so far haven't produced more successful or happier kids.

By many accounts, they've done just the opposite.

More than 1.3 million American students drop out of high school each year, while nearly half of those enrolling in college leave without a degree. In recent years, U.S. teens have ranked twenty-fifth among thirty-four industrialized nations on international exams in math and science, a pattern that dates back several years. Corporate officials meanwhile complain that young job applicants lack key twenty-first-century skills, such as critical thinking and creativity, and that they can't work in teams or effectively communicate their ideas.

Student morale is in equally dismal shape. Anxiety, depression, and drug and alcohol abuse are on the rise, while increasing numbers of kids are taking stimulants in hopes of boosting their test scores and grades.

The more that Americans hear of these problems, the more we also hear about supposed global education superstars—led in recent years by Finland, and including China, Singapore, and South Korea—who regularly outperform U.S. children on those international tests. Experts tell us we must look to what those countries are doing to help our kids survive in an increasingly competitive world economy.

This strikes me as terribly misguided. We don't need to travel that far for solutions to our education predicaments.

We have all the answers we need right here at home.

We've had them, in fact, for more than one hundred years.

To best explain what I mean, I'd like to show you how our school employs proven teaching techniques from America's past that hold enormous promise for our nation's future. That's why I invite you to accompany me now, down the sidewalk that leads from a busy Oakland intersection and past the row of overgrown hedges and chain-link fence approaching our wrought-iron front gate.

I promise to be mindful of your time, as I must be of my own. In August 2013, doctors diagnosed me with stage IV bone cancer and told me that I have, at most, another year to live. It's no exaggeration to say I feel some urgency to finish this book, which I've been working on in fits and starts for nearly twenty years. My purpose isn't to leave behind a record of my own life's work. Instead, I'm proposing that the formula behind Park Day School and similar schools' success can help solve America's most pressing education dilemmas, while putting the joy back into learning.

The gate is open.

Let's get started.

THE TOUR BEGINS

Our small private school has an old-fashioned look, considering its location on the expanding frontier of Silicon Valley, near

Pixar Studios and the University of California at Berkeley. The tall pines and giant magnolia in the courtyard have stood here even longer than the Spanish-style stucco-and-tile building—designed in 1928 and originally used as an orphanage—which now houses most of our classrooms. Yet should you linger here at recess or during the lunch hour, what will really take you back in time is the way the kids behave.

You'll rarely see a child standing alone. Instead, kids line up to hang on the monkey bars, walk hand-in-hand or with arms circling each others' backs, or kneel together to check out the progress of the carrots in our garden or the chickens in our coop. Even our oldest students, who by this age at other schools would be standing around in self-conscious cliques, often chase each other around the old wooden gazebo. They're likely to be playing a game of tag they call "Manhunt": acting, in other words, like the children they still are.

Now stroll through our hallways, and, please, feel free to peek inside the classrooms. The first thing that may strike you is that our students are usually out of their chairs. Unlike the vast majority of public schools and even most private schools today, we strictly ban the standardized tests mandated in public schools, which allows lots of extra time for hands-on learning. You'll be less likely to see teachers lecturing or students sitting quietly in rows than to find kids mixing ingredients to produce non-toxic household cleaners, or designing a rainwater catchment system for the school, or grinding wheat to cook muffins for lunch. Some may be acting out a drama they've written, playing the parts of space travelers or inventors, while others huddle in a group, learning how to use a compass by designing a compass rose. Reliably, some will be sprawling on a rug or lounging in overstuffed chairs, holding class meetings or reading to each other.

If you stick around long enough, you'll understand why Harvard University researchers have chosen to visit our school four times a year to study creativity in children. We're proud that Park Day School is a place where in an endlessly hurried world, kids have precious leisure time for creativity—and community.

IT TAKES OUR VILLAGE

Oakland is one of America's most crime-ridden cities, ranking first in the nation in recent years for robbery and car theft, and among the top ten U.S. cities for murder. Even so, Park Day School is known as a place where a dramatically diverse group of people manage, year after year, to get along.

Our parent body has included firefighters, day-care workers, several best-selling authors, mechanics, graphic artists, food stamp recipients, journalists, and university professors. That means our students come from various socio-economic backgrounds and bring a richness of ethnic, religious, and gender diversity. We are deliberate in our efforts to have diverse families because it is valuable for everyone to share the multiple stories of their lives with each other and to bridge the divides that often occur in society.

More than 90 percent of our graduates attend college, compared to barely 68 percent nationwide, and they've gone on from there to careers as engineers, lawyers, business owners, social workers, actors, artists, and chefs. We also claim a Chilean pop star, a couple of successful authors, and a higher than average share of non-profit employees, including the current chief of staff of the Sierra Club, and—we're especially proud of this— several teachers, at least three university professors, and two public school principals.

Among our recent alumnae are two boys with extraordinary

stories. Lasana Lapia, born in Sierra Leone, was adopted by an American couple after his mother was killed and he was bitten on the leg by a venomous cobra. Saleh Khalaf, born in Iraq, was flown in for treatment at Oakland Children's Hospital after he picked up a bright yellow cluster bomb, thinking it was a toy, and lost both his hands and one eye. As I'll later elaborate, the school gave both boys a refuge as they underwent surgery for their life-threatening injuries and healed from emotional and physical traumas, while they, in turn, gave their fellow classmates unforgettable lessons in courage and resilience.

That sort of exchange tells a lot about the strength of our small community, and how important it is for us to *be* a strong community. It's a value that lies at the heart of what I'll later be describing in detail: that countercultural as it may seem these days, ample scientific research has now confirmed that trustworthy relationships aren't frills in our nation's race to compete in the global economy. In fact, they're essential for a quality education.

It's all part of our modern dilemma. As Americans become ever more disconnected from their own extended families, religious institutions, and clubs, our schools have been left to serve as the centers of society. It's here, unlike anywhere else, after all, where families are legally bound, at least for a few years, to show up on a regular basis. Moreover, it's here where some of the most intimate and wrenching family problems first surface: where teachers may discover that a girl has been cutting herself or that a boy has been physically abused. It's also here where most parents first learn that their child has a serious learning or behavioral problem that may powerfully affect the rest of his or her life. Finally, it's here where a family may have their best chance of discovering effective ways to cope.

Over the years, I've grown comfortable with the notion of a

school as a secular ministry—and with my role as its virtual village pastor—despite my somewhat checkered past as a former altar boy who has not attended mass for more than forty years. All the same, even I have been surprised over the years by the way our families have turned to me in times of crisis. I've been called on to deliver eulogies at half a dozen funerals of parents and students, some of them held right here at school. Similarly, it came as no surprise to most of our families that on the day of the 9/11 terrorist attacks, when many other local schools sent students home early, we kept our doors open, as families flocked in to seek comfort with one another.

A PIECE OF CAKE

I arrived at the site of the experiment that was to become Park Day School in July 1976, as a twenty-two-year-old graduate student, sporting a large red Afro, bushy mustache, and braces on my teeth.

It was a time of great excitement about the possibilities of public education. An anti-authoritarian mood that had grown in the wake of the Vietnam War was challenging the status quo in schools. Teaching institutions were rediscovering the decades-old works of the developmental psychologists Jean Piaget, from Switzerland, who said, "Education means making creators. . . . You have to make inventors, innovators—not conformists," and Lev Vygotsky, from Belarus, who said, "People with great passions, people who accomplish great deeds, people who possess strong feelings, even people with great minds and a strong personality, rarely come out of good little boys and girls."

"Child-centered" strategies were newly in vogue. In a trend imported from Great Britain in the late 1960s, some U.S.

schools were building classrooms without walls, in which students could wander between "learning stations," following their interests. As part of my teaching credential program at San Francisco State, I was working with a visionary public schoolteacher named Roni Howard, whose sixth-grade classroom was a wonderland of attractions, including a large enclosed wooden maze, designed and built by the eleven-year-olds, to train a group of Norway rats.

In Oakland, a group of ambitious parents and teachers had just split off from another private school and were setting up a classroom of their own at the Beth Jacob Orthodox Jewish Synagogue on Park Boulevard, the street from which our school would later take its name. The new director, Gerri Shapiro, had heard of me from my college adviser and asked if I could "help out."

"We can't pay you," she said.

I came anyway. And after just one day spent painting the walls of the new school, I was hooked for the rest of my career.

The chief lure, at that point, was my first meeting with Susan Erb, a founding teacher of the new school, and, as I was soon to realize, one of the most talented educators I've ever known. Tall and willowy, Susan conveys a serene confidence with adults that quickly morphs into gentle wackiness with a young child. When speaking with children, she'll rarely look down at them; instead, she squats or kneels to address them at eye-level, as she calls their attention to wonders they haven't yet noticed. She has convinced several generations of young students that fairies live in the trees in the courtyard—the children write notes to them, which always receive answers—and decorates her first-grade classroom with a "magic detector," a small disco ball that she turns on, illuminating every corner of her classroom, as a ritual to start each day.

I realized right away that serving as Susan's apprentice would teach me more than anything I'd learn in graduate school. So I quit the program and took a chance that the volunteer work might lead to a paid job.

As the weeks passed, Susan and I were joined by another gifted teacher, Harriet Cohen, who by our good fortune had spotted a want-ad for a teacher posted at the YMCA. Harriet had a master's degree in music from Smith College and had taught kindergarten in Spanish Harlem in New York. She brought a love of the arts and a particularly strong sense of social justice to her work with the children, and so deeply shared our passion for teaching that the three of us became a long-lasting nucleus for the school. Together, we maintained a continuity of spirit amid changing management and settings in those early years, remaining together at Park Day School for the next three decades. After Harriet retired in 2009, she continued to work as a substitute teacher at Park Day as well as at Emerson Elementary, a nearby public school, well into her seventies.

Back then, of course, I had no idea what the next thirty years were to bring. The summer was soon over, and by September we had finished painting, visited Dumpsters for cast-off furniture, and appealed to established schools for books they might be ready to give away. Gerri, our director, and her hastily assembled board of parents had corralled a group of twenty-two children and each contributed funds which barely covered our initial expenses. They let me teach the occasional class, but I was still working without pay.

All this time, Susan, Harriet, and I were talking constantly about the kind of school and community we wanted to create. We still joke today about how, every once in a while, as we were setting up the classrooms, we'd try to catch Gerri's ear as she rushed by, to ask about her plans for the new curriculum.

"Piece of cake!" was all she ever said, implying that this was the least of our challenges.

And so we made things up, creating lesson plans and routines and minting traditions from whim, serendipity, and necessity. Our cramped classroom and limited resources pushed us outside on frequent field trips, as did the synagogue's requirement that we vacate the classrooms every Friday afternoon to make room for Shabbat celebrations. We got in the habit of holding Friday classes in a nearby park, which is why some students from those years mistakenly think that's how we got our name.

By October of our first year as a school, we had expanded our enrollment to twenty-eight. I was given my own class to teach, and finally got my first paycheck.

We moved locations twice over the next six years, expanding our enrollment tenfold and finally settling into our current site at the former orphanage. In 1986, at the age of thirty-two, I was chosen to lead the school. My hair has since turned white, and I now keep it cut short. I celebrated my sixtieth birthday in November, coinciding with my retirement—an event that, were it not for my illness, I would have happily put off indefinitely.

Over nearly forty years, I've watched hundreds of uncivilized kindergartners grow into interesting, thoughtful teens, and seen many a nervous parent become more confident. All the while, our small private school has increasingly cultivated a public mission. We not only practice our values on our campus but make an effort to explain them to the wider world. As our Web site says: "We believe a successful learner is one who is confident, caring, and creative. We believe success is measured by a student's ability to define his or her place in the world, guided by intellectual skills and a social perspective."

In practice, of course, we are much more specific in the way we face the challenges weighing on all American schools today.

In an era of teaching to the test, we've chosen to focus our energy on higher-minded goals. We believe our students will lead more productive and fulfilled lives as resilient collaborators than as insecure competitors. As school curricula become increasingly standardized, we encourage a love of learning by recognizing and responding to students' individual interests. And in an age when young people are too often cynics, we prioritize social awareness and activism.

None of these policies has interfered with our students earning high GPAs and test scores once they enter high school. Often, they excel compared to students who've been burned out by years of high-stakes exams. Many are accepted by top colleges—with most, even more important, finding colleges that fit their interests and needs—and go on to interesting and satisfying lives.

Thus, if what we offer them in grade school truly seems countercultural, I'd say it's time to reconsider what we want from our culture.

THE FORMULA

As I've mentioned, throughout our early history at Park Day, we thought we were making it all up. None of us knew there was a formula for our success. We followed our best instincts, improvising away, creating and adding strategies as we found they proved successful in building a strong community of learners. Yet in everything we did, we held true to three main principles: we considered children's emotional needs and development just as seriously as their academic progress; we worked to build a strong, supportive community; and we encouraged students to develop a sense of social justice.

Then, in 1995, I happened to attend an educational conference where I learned that what have become some of Park Day's core strategies in fact belong to a long and honorable, homegrown American pedagogical tradition. Its name is Progressive Education, and it emerged during the Progressive Era, at the turn of the twentieth century, one of the most tumultuous and hopeful periods in our nation's history. My interest soon led me to Lawrence Cremin's classic history of Progressive Education, *The Transformation of the School: Progressivism in American Education, 1876–1957.* I have since read and reread this tome, taking careful notes, and buying extra copies to press on my colleagues. Eventually I delved into my own research, inspired by Cremin's scholarship, and learned that long before the "Open Classroom" movement of the late 1970s and '80s, which everyone then seemed to think was new and revolutionary, dedicated progressive educators, their work all but buried by history, had originally forged this path. They had designed schools to engage children's emotions as well as their intellects, just as we had done. Similarly, they'd built strong and caring communities, and encouraged children's sense of social justice.

The more I learned, the more I was struck by the parallels between those reformers' efforts and our work at Park Day. My colleagues shared my enthusiasm, and soon we were proudly referring to our school as "progressive," as we learned more about our roots, and reached out to other schools that shared our values.

What I learned next was less encouraging.

A dominant force in American schools up until World War II, Progressive Education subsequently suffered a demonized decline. Some critics charged the schools were being run by leftists; others called them overly permissive. Alas, both charges stuck. Today, only a few dozen schools scattered throughout

America—including several established a hundred years ago and many others founded after the 1960s—still call themselves "progressive." Many others may be progressive in nature but shy away from using the historically tainted name. What's left are hundreds of thousands of other schools, public and private, that may employ bits and pieces of our legacy, but only a small minority of students who benefit from the comprehensive and intentional plans in use at schools like Park Day.

America's relatively tiny scattering of explicitly progressive schools is made up of mostly small, independent organizations on the west and east coasts, together with a handful of public and charter schools. A few can be found in the South and several in the Midwest, including an entire public school district that calls itself "progressive," just outside of Chicago. To be sure, anyone who thinks Progressive Education need be limited to cozy private enclaves should consider the models of several flourishing progressive public schools, such as the acclaimed Mission Hill School pilot public school in inner-city Boston; the Odyssey Charter School in Altadena, California; PS 87 in Manhattan; the Wickliffe Elementary School in Upper Arlington, Ohio; and the Namaste Charter School in southwest Chicago. These popular public schools prove that our methods don't require extraordinary infusions of money, nor do they depend on homogenous, affluent students, although they certainly do require well-trained and motivated teachers.

Unfortunately, however, the word "progressive" remains tangled up in the public's perception with leftist politics, while progressive schools continue to be caricaturized as permissive, "loosey-goosey," "touchy-feely," and even "crunchy granola," to the point that many of the minority of Americans who have heard of Progressive Education consider it passé, at best. Amid our current worries that students above all need more "rigor" and "basics," the stigma is so strong that even some of the most dedicated progressive educators I know have reached the point of making sly references to the "p-word" while jumping on the bandwagon of rebranding trademark progressive pedagogical methods with bland names such as "21st Century Learning."

To me, this is beyond unfortunate. The trend threatens our identity and the coherence of our educational methods precisely when we're justifiably poised for a renaissance. American students today need our values and strategies more than ever, and, unlike before, we've got the evidence to prove their efficacy. Abundant research shows that three core classroom strategies invented by progressive educators—namely, letting students pursue their own interests (now commonly referred to as "inquiry-based" education); using a multidisciplinary approach to teaching skills and content; and organizing material into student projects ("project-based learning")—are extraordinarily effective ways to develop the skills we most need in the new global economy. Scientists have also shown that our traditional emphasis on building strong school communities helps young people avoid risky behaviors such as substance abuse and sexual promiscuity.

All this helps explain why now is no time for progressive educators to turn our backs on our legacy. We need to stop tolerating misinformed critics misdefining what we do, and instead, speak out about the benefits we see in our classrooms every day—benefits that should rightly be the legacy of millions of American children. Until we do, Progressive Education will continue to be the buried treasure of American education: the all but exclusive privilege of a tiny minority of our nation's most wealthy and influential families.

Here's what I mean: In recent years, Silicon Valley moguls (including the late Steve Jobs), top-level national politicians, and a large coterie of other Hollywood film and TV stars including Matt Damon, Dustin Hoffman, Kiefer Sutherland, Mark Hamill, Julia Louis-Dreyfus, Meg Ryan, and Dennis Quaid, have all sent their children to progressive schools. The former California governor Arnold Schwarzenegger, and his former wife, Maria Shriver, gave such support to one progressive public school in Woodland Hills, California, that it renamed itself the Chime Institute Schwarzenegger Community School. With rare exceptions, however, these privileged parents never discuss their choices in public. And whether their concern is privacy, politics, or fear of being judged or envied for the wealth that makes their choices possible, the result is the same: the appreciation of some of our nation's most valuable educational innovations remains mostly an elitist perk.

This silence—at a time when America is so hungry for models of schools that work to improve both hearts and minds—is particularly poignant when it comes to the case of President Barack Obama, who himself attended a progressive private school, the Punahou School in Honolulu. The Obamas went on to enroll their daughters in progressive private schools: first, the Laboratory Schools at the University of Chicago in Hyde Park, founded by the Progressive Education pioneer John Dewey, and then the Sidwell Friends School in Washington, a Quaker school which doesn't call itself progressive but which meets all the criteria. Education Secretary Arne Duncan also attended the Lab Schools, as have the children of former Obama chief of staff and current Chicago mayor Rahm Emanuel.

Obama's alma mater, the Punahou School, founded in 1841, is the oldest and one of the largest independent schools in America, with 3,750 K–12 students as of this writing. While the school today doesn't explicitly call itself progressive—"innovative" is its brand of choice—its roots tell a different story. Dewey himself

visited the school for six weeks in 1951, enrolling his two children there during that time. In a recent interview, school president Jim Scott described the school as a "very progressive place."
(The school even has its own Center for Public Service, modeled after similar centers at top college campuses, where students and families can apply for volunteer work.)

Obama's family wasn't wealthy during his years at Punahou.
Like 20 percent of the student body today, he benefited from
financial aid. Nor was Obama, at least initially, a model student; according to his memoir, *Dreams from My Father*, he at
first slacked off with friends, got poor grades, smoked mari-
juana, and even tried cocaine. Yet Obama's years at Punahou
were transformative, in part as a result of the school's progressive character. On a December 2004 visit to the school shortly
before being sworn in to the U.S. Senate, Obama credited his
teachers with spotting potential beyond what he was then able
to demonstrate in the classroom, giving him encouragement
that helped him later excel at Columbia University and Harvard Law School.

LOVING LEARNING

My hope for this book is that it will help allow millions of other
American students to share just this sort of opportunity—to be
recognized and nurtured in ways that help them reach their
highest potential. In contrast to the current popular ideal of
stern instruction, pushing children to perform in ways that can
be measured by computers reading filled-in bubbles, this is
teaching that awakens a love of learning, a strengthening of
character, and an elicitation of curiosity. Not least, it's a lot more
fun. Because without some kind of positive motivation, how can

we possibly expect that our children would want to go on learning for the rest of their lives?

Jonathan Berk, a professor of finance who teaches a course on Critical and Analytical Thinking at Stanford University's School of Business, has thought deeply about this idea ever since he observed his two daughters at Park Day School several years ago. That experience changed the way he thinks about education, he says, convincing him that students learn best when they're experiencing joy.

"I don't mean joy where you take a ride and feel good," he explained. "I mean the joy you get from working hard and mastering things. There's no greater happiness than struggling and mastering."

As a nation, we used to be familiar with this wisdom. It is part of our American heritage.

So, how did we come to forget?

CHAPTER 1

"Remakers of Mankind"

Wickliffe Elementary School, in a suburb of Columbus, Ohio, is one of America's few public schools that remain unabashedly progressive.   Photograph by Julie Eirich-Parker

> *That there was need for the reaction, indeed for a revolt, seems to me*
> *unquestionable.* —JOHN DEWEY (1859–1952)

WHAT A DIFFERENCE *EMILE* MAKES

In 1762, the Romantic philosopher Jean-Jacques Rousseau published a surprisingly incendiary novel: *Emile, or On Education.* His challenge to conventional wisdom about how children should be schooled continues to roil debate today.

Written in the voice of a tutor describing his vision of an ideal education for an "imaginary" student named Emile, the book recommends dispensing with texts and a preordained course of study to allow the child, during his early years, to discover the world through his senses. Only through an education "adapted to the human heart," Rousseau suggested, could the child's innate intelligence and basic goodness remain uncorrupted.

Now, one might reasonably question—as many have done for centuries—Rousseau's competence to preach about the care of young children. His mother had died nine days after his birth, and his father abandoned him ten years later, leaving him to educate himself. In his *Confessions*, he revealed that he later persuaded his mistress, the mother of four of his babies, to surrender the infants to an orphanage, writing: "I trembled at the thought of intrusting them to a family ill-brought up, to be still worse educated."

Even so, Rousseau wrote with iconoclastic confidence about his vision of the right way to guide youthful spirits, from urging mothers to breastfeed their own children—a radical idea at the time—to prescribing that all young boys learn a trade. And *Emile* had a tremendous impact far outside Rousseau's native city-state of Geneva. The German philosopher Immanuel Kant wrote that he had read the book several times, declaring it "a contribution to the restoration of the rights of mankind." At the same time, Rousseau infuriated both Protestants and the Catholic Church by his rejection of religious doctrines, including original sin and divine revelation. The archbishop of Paris condemned him; his books were burned, and he was forced to flee Geneva under the threat of arrest. He traveled through Europe for the next twelve years, in declining health, and died of a hemorrhage while staying on a friend's estate near Paris.

The spirit of *Emile* has outlived him, however—for two and a half centuries, and counting.

In 1798, a failed Swiss farmer named Johann Heinrich Pestalozzi drew inspiration from *Emile* as he reinvented himself as an educational scientist. Challenging the rote instruction becoming prevalent in his day, Pestalozzi, who has since been hailed as the father of modern educational science, founded schools in Switzerland and Germany that were dedicated to learning by "heart, head, and hand." Rather than memorizing lessons, children in these schools sang, drew, wrote, and performed calisthenics. A few decades later, in Germany, one of Pestalozzi's students, Friedrich Wilhelm August Froebel, coined the word *Kindergarten* ("garden of children") for his own idyllic school where the youngest students played with geometrical building blocks that Froebel invented, in what he called their "free work." It was through this lineage that Rousseau's rebellious notion of a kinder, gentler education inspired American education reformers who emerged toward the beginning of the twentieth century.

This was the heyday of America's celebrated Progressive Era, lasting roughly from 1870 to 1920. It coincided with what historians would later refer to as the Second Industrial Revolution, a flurry of technologically driven social change. Cars, bicycles, petrochemicals, railways, light bulbs, and radios were transforming every aspect of daily life, as Americans, together with millions of new immigrants, were flooding into the cities. Overnight, it seemed, work was moving out of the family home and farm and into newly built factories.

As urban populations increased, so did poverty and crime. State politicians who were mainly concerned with assimilating and stabilizing the masses embraced compulsory schools, which gradually replaced what had been a haphazard system of impoverished families schooling their children at home or in one-room schoolhouses, while wealthier families hired private tutors or sent their sons to boarding academies. By the turn of the century, thirty-four states had enacted laws that made school attendance mandatory until age fourteen. By 1920, more than two thirds of American children were attending school.

The majority of these new institutions, known as "common schools," had been inspired by Prussia's education system, in which schools both looked and operated like factories, with strict routines marked off by the ringing of bells. The new idea was that all students should be taught a common content—in broad concept not unlike the Common Core standards now being adopted by the majority of American states, but in practice much more basic and less interesting.

Judging from news reports from that time, most of these schools were uncommonly awful. Fifty or more children of varying ages might be crowded into a single room, seated at rows of desks that were bolted to the floor, as they parroted back an instructor's promptings. Teachers disciplined boys and girls alike by beating them with canes. "That there was need for the reaction, indeed for a revolt, seems to me unquestionable," the philosopher and psychologist John Dewey, the most celebrated leader of the reformists, would later recall. "The evils of the traditional, conventional schoolroom, its almost complete isolation from actual life, and the deadly depression of mind which the weight of formal material caused, all cried out for reform."

The dismal state of so many of the common schools was first exposed in 1892 in a series of magazine articles written by the muckraking journalist Joseph Mayer Rice. The former pediatrician had given up his clinical practice after deciding that children's welfare would be best improved by better care of their environment. He surveyed public schools in thirty-six cities, from the east coast to the Midwest, chronicling the prisonlike conditions. "It is indeed incomprehensible," he wrote, "that so many loving mothers . . . are willing, without hesitation, to resign the fate of their little ones to the tender mercies of ward politicians, who in many instances have no scruples in placing the children in class-rooms the atmosphere of which is not fit for human beings to breathe, and in charge of teachers who treat them with a degree of severity that borders on barbarism."

While determinedly chronicling the worst of public education, however, Rice also highlighted cases in which a few brave pioneers, whom he called "progressive," were experimenting with a more enlightened type of instruction, and, in many cases, creating islands of excellence. In Indiana, for instance, schools were introducing drawing, painting, and clay modeling, while teaching pupils "to be helpful to each other." Rice also took special note of the Cook County Normal School, outside of Chicago, where Colonel Francis W. Parker, whom Dewey himself would later hail as the father of Progressive Education, had attracted international notice for his "all-side" education of children, which included classes in art, nature study, and social relations.

Rice's groundbreaking articles informed and mobilized educators and parents, who from then on increasingly insisted on replacing the prevailing authoritarian discipline and mindless drills with more uplifting practices.

What they wanted, in other words, was to start treating American kids more like Rousseau's Emile.

AN EXPLOSION OF SCIENCE AND REFORM

These early rebellions in favor of more humane schools took place in one of the most energetic, idealistic, and transformational periods of history, during which all sorts of new creative ideas were emerging in America and beyond. During just three of these exceptional decades, from 1890 to 1920, William James wrote the first treatises on the new science of psychology; Orville Wright flew the first American airplane; and Henry Ford invented the Model T. In Europe, Albert Einstein developed his theory of relativity; Sigmund Freud published his *Interpretation of Dreams*; Igor Stravinsky composed his revolutionary *Rite of Spring*; and Pablo Picasso painted his proto-Cubist *Les Demoiselles d'Avignon*.

While scientists and artists were challenging convention, so was a new breed of middle-class activists with novel ideas about fairness. Women were demanding the vote; the celebrated muckraking journalists Ida Tarbell and Upton Sinclair were exposing corruption by Standard Oil and the meatpacking industry; and trade unions were calling for reductions in the seventy-to-eighty-hour workweek.

Many in this new generation of activists turned their focus to the treatment of children, inspired by findings from the brand-new science of psychology as to how young minds develop. No longer were children considered merely miniature, uncivilized adults. A new sense of their vulnerability and also of their capacity for rehabilitation informed challenges to the common practices of child labor and sentencing juvenile delinquents as adults. The first juvenile court was established in Cook County, Illinois, in 1899, guided by the revolutionary idea that the government could and should seek to turn youths' lives around, rather than merely punish them.

It was only natural that these reformers eventually took on the draconian public schools of their time. The new schools they created banned corporal punishment in favor of encouraging students' allegiances to a wholly new sort of school, which Francis Parker envisioned as "a model home, a complete community and embryonic democracy." As superintendent of schools in Quincy, Massachusetts, Parker, a stern-looking, bald man with a large handlebar mustache, replaced rote learning and grades with more spontaneous approaches, including group projects and art classes. He won fame in 1879 for his "Quincy Method," after his students surpassed peers in other schools on state tests.

While Dewey and Parker remain the two most famous names among American progressive reformers, the movement was heavily populated—and certainly in some cases, led—by some exceptionally strong-minded women, many of whose schools are still operating today. They include Marietta Johnson, founder of the School of Organic Education, in Fairhope, Alabama, in 1907; Caroline Pratt, founder of the City and Country School in New York City, in 1913; Agnes Hocking, a co-founder of the Shady Hill School in Cambridge, Massachusetts, in 1915; and Lucy Sprague Mitchell, founder of the Bank Street School for Children, in Manhattan, in 1916.

Of course, if you judge only by the sheer number of schools that are still operating today, the most influential of all of this era's Progressive reformers, man or woman, was the Italian physician Maria Montessori. In 1906, Montessori, a medical doctor who had advocated for more enlightened treatment and education of mentally ill and delinquent youth, was invited to oversee the education of a group of children from low-income families in a new apartment building in Rome. There she established the first Casa dei Bambini, a school for more than fifty children between the ages of two and seven, and the precursor of what today are an estimated 20,000 Montessori schools in more than fifty-two nations, including Russia and Cambodia.

Google founders Larry Page and Sergey Brin both attended Montessori schools—and have credited them as contributing to their success—while other famously creative alumni include Albert Einstein, Anne Frank, Julia Child, and the Nobel Prize–winning author Gabriel García Márquez. American inventors Alexander Graham Bell and Thomas Edison helped create Montessori schools in Canada and the United States. And Bill and Hillary Clinton sent their daughter Chelsea to one.

Montessori, like the American reformers, was strongly influenced by Rousseau, Froebel, and Pestalozzi. Her famous injunction to "follow the child" expressed her own determined departure from regimented schools teaching by rote memorization, and toward a more joyful form of learning largely driven by a student's curiosity. Dewey and Montessori solidly agreed on these basics but diverged on other issues, including the age at which children should be taught to read (Dewey favored waiting until eight, whereas Montessori thought they were ready at four or five) and the degree of freedom children should have in their play (Dewey and his followers found Montessori too restrictive), which contributed to keeping the two movements from officially merging. While many of the estimated 4,000 Montessori schools in America today explicitly call themselves "progressive," others avoid that distinction.

Something similar happened with the Waldorf schools—the first of which was founded for children of the workers at the Waldorf Astoria cigarette company in Stuttgart, Germany, in 1919, under the influence of the Austrian philosopher and architect Rudolf Steiner. Along with Dewey and Montessori, Steiner also rebelled against the claustrophobic nature of the schools of his time, and developed a more humanistic alternative that offered children less academic pressure and more freedom. In 2014, there were estimated to be more than 3,000 Waldorf schools and kindergartens in 60 countries, with about 150 such schools in the United States. Like the Montessori schools, Waldorf schools are in many important ways remarkably similar to the ones Dewey inspired—including in their rejection of standardized tests and grades, their emphasis on building strong relationships among students and teachers, and their interest in nurturing idealism. Yet they remain a separate movement, and, unlike the Montessori schools, relatively few Waldorf schools describe themselves as "progressive."

One important divergence was a spiritual element in Steiner's philosophy, known as "anthroposophy," which includes the belief in angels. (Waldorf proponents respond to critics by saying the schools don't teach religion.) Waldorf schools are also distinguished by their relatively strong emphasis on nurturing a child's imagination. To this end, they don't formally teach reading until age seven. Also, while both progressive and Montessori schools leave decisions about popular media up to individual families, and Waldorf schools strictly discourage exposure to TV and video games in the early grades, while often waiting until high school to bring computers into the classroom.

It's striking that long before the age of instant digital communication and globalization, visionaries in America and Europe were simultaneously reacting in such similar ways against the early public schools of their times. They created hardy models that continue to appeal to today's humanists all over the world. Recently, in fact, I learned of a reform movement in China, where education experts are rebelling against the modern, test-driven culture and looking for alternative models that might better nurture future innovators—and where better to look, they argue, than America's progressive schools?

HEARTS AND MINDS

America's twentieth-century reformers were nothing if not earnest. "If I should tell you any secret of my life," Colonel Francis Parker wrote, "it is the intense desire I have to see growth and improvement in human beings."

As much as they wore their hearts on their sleeves, however, the crusaders prided themselves on their allegiance to science, culling ideas from research from all over the world and exhaustively testing their hypotheses and methods. In 1896, seventeen years after the Quincy Method first made news, Dewey, an extraordinarily prodigious writer and commentator (his works have been collected in thirty-seven volumes), established his Laboratory Schools as a center of research and demonstration for the Department of Pedagogy at the University of Chicago. (Just in case you're wondering, John Dewey didn't also invent the Dewey decimal system—that was Melvil Dewey, no relation, in 1876.)

In Chicago, John Dewey tested and showcased several strategies introduced by Parker, including hands-on activities, interdisciplinary instruction, and hefty doses of physical exercise, music, art, and practical skills including home economics and carpentry. Through careful supervision of the students, and lots of trial and error, he sought to devise a new academic curriculum that as much as possible would break down the barriers between the classroom and the world outside, making school more like "real life."

Carleton W. Washburne, one of Dewey's most dedicated disciples and the celebrated superintendent of schools in Winnetka, Illinois, from 1919 to 1943, was, like Dewey, a daring innovator who was also a great believer in using research to inform new practices. Washburne established a formal research department for his district, which eventually published more than a hundred articles in education journals. In 1930, he also embarked on a remarkable journey with his family and one of the principals of his schools to investigate educational innovations in Japan, China, India, Turkey, and Russia. He compiled his research in a book that he titled *Remakers of Mankind*. (Among other observations, Washburne noted his surprise at the emphasis on individual thinking in Chinese schools of the 1930s, despite loyalty to Confucian ethics. Dewey's ideas were then popular in China, where the goal of education under Sun Yat-sen, as Washburne wrote, was freedom of the individual—a marked contrast with the uniformity he witnessed in ultranationalist Japan.)

Many of these early reformers' innovations endure today in mainstream schools. To cite just a few examples, modern students can thank Dewey, Parker, Washburne, and their followers for playgrounds, jungle gyms, field trips, and art and music classes, in addition to morning assemblies and community service.

ROLLER-COASTER YEARS

The Progressive Education movement reached its peak of influence in the late 1930s and 1940s. In 1938, a cover story in *Time* magazine declared that the movement had grown in just twenty years from a "tiny and, in many eyes, a crackpot movement quarantined in a handful of private schools" to claiming strongholds in the suburbs of New York, Chicago, and Los Angeles, to the point that "no U.S. school has completely escaped its influence."

A few years later, the movement gained considerable prestige from the erroneously named "Eight-Year Study": a landmark longitudinal research project which in fact lasted from 1930 to

1940. University-based scholars directed by a commission of the Progressive Education Association, the movement's then powerful trade association, followed 1,475 students from 30 progressive and other innovative schools from high school to college and compared them with an equal number of carefully matched students from traditional schools. They found that the students from the non-traditional schools had earned higher grades, demonstrated more leadership, won more academic honors, cared more about books and art, and revealed a better understanding of democracy than their peers.

By the late 1930s, the Progressive Education Association's conferences were drawing 5,000 people at a time, which would be an extraordinary feat for an educational organization in our own age. Major universities trained teachers in its methods.

The movement was never really monolithic, however, and its semblance of unity was already beginning to crack. By 1927, Dewey had become alarmed by how some overenthusiastic followers were completely eclipsing the role of the teacher as they strove to attend more to the interests of the child. Even Emile's tutor had never entirely surrendered control of his tiny classroom. But as Dewey wrote, some educators by then were merely placing students in rooms full of toys and tools and letting them respond "according to their own desires." He called that practice "really stupid," adding that "it misconceives the conditions of independent thinking."

Another fracture emerged along political lines. In the early years of the Great Depression, opposing factions of reformers squabbled over whether schools should take on the role of trying to create a more just society by instilling political values in their students. The conflict famously came to a head at a 1932 conference, when George Counts, then a professor at the Teachers College at Columbia University, gave a series of speeches later published as a booklet entitled *Dare the School Build a New Social Order?* Counts's demand for more political activism alienated many members of the Progressive Education Association, who wanted to keep schools focused on responding to individual children's emotional and academic needs.

Counts, a leading trade unionist, went on to become president of the American Federation of Teachers in 1939, after which he founded the New York State Liberal Party and ran unsuccessfully for the U.S. Senate. Throughout these years, and especially after World War II, as Americans became steadily more politically conservative, Progressive Education's public ties with Counts and other left-leaning activists weakened popular support for the alternative schools.

Following John Dewey's death in 1952, critics made much of Dewey's outspoken sympathies for labor and the socialist People's Lobby, of which he served as president (he referred to the major political parties as "the errand boys of big business"). Conservative education experts favored keeping all discussion of ideology out of American classrooms. They also charged that the progressives' focus on the arts and social relationships was squeezing out time for the "three Rs" of a classic education. As described by a group of critics calling themselves the Essentialists, led by Columbia's Teachers College professor William Chandler Bagley, the reformers were turning children into poor spellers and, overall, making U.S. education "effeminate."

To truly understand just how low the once influential movement had sunk in the popular consciousness by 1955, however, you would need only to page through Patrick Dennis's novel published that year, *Auntie Mame: An Irreverent Escapade*, which later became a popular play and movie. The heart of the book features an argument between Mame and her nephew's guardian, who objects to Mame having sent the boy to a "progressive" school.

"I walk into that so-called 'institution of learning'—and what do I find? A whole schoolroom of them—boys, girls, teachers— romping around, stark-naked, bare as the day they were born!" rages the guardian.

It gets worse. The nephew then explains that the class had been playing a game called "fish families," in which the boys and girls pretend to be fish, depositing and fertilizing eggs in the sand.

"What could be more wholesome and natural?" Mame demands.

Clearly, Dennis didn't expect his readers to agree.

The Progressive Education Association dissolved that very year, depriving the reformers of an organized way to respond to increasing criticism. But the *coup de grâce* came two years later, when the Soviet Union launched its Sputnik satellite, fanning popular fears that American children were falling behind their superpower rivals in math and science. After that, the new demands for a "back to basics" education became irresistible.

In 1965, the Elementary and Secondary Education Act required standardized testing in public schools. The spirit of *Emile* was in full retreat.

This was the context for the schools of my formative years, in the late 1950s and early 1960s.

A MODEL EDUCATION—OF WHAT *NOT* TO DO

My lifelong passion for Progressive Education emerged directly from my experience with its antithesis.

From kindergarten through high school, I attended strict Catholic schools in a working-class neighborhood of San Francisco. Our crowded classrooms, with their immobile desks, might as well have been teleported from the early 1900s, when Dewey wrote:

> *Just as the biologist can take a bone or two and reconstruct the whole animal, so, if we put before the mind's eye the ordinary school room, with its rows of ugly desks placed in geometrical order, crowded together so that there shall be as little moving room as possible, desks almost all of the same size, with just space enough to hold books, pencils and paper, and add a table, some chairs, the bare walls, and possibly a few pictures, we can reconstruct the only educational activity that can possibly go on in such a place. It is made for listening— because simply studying lessons out of a book is only another kind of listening; it marks the dependency of one mind upon another . . . it means, comparatively speaking, passivity. . . .*

We students lived in fear of the nuns who glared out from the shadows of their black-and-white habits. Several of my teachers would slap a child's face at the slightest provocation, interpreting the merest eyeroll as insolence. While I never got hit myself, I watched others being pulled by their hair and ears, grabbed by their necks, and in the case of one minor smart aleck, thrown across the room.

Now, Catholic schools have always had a special reputation for sternness. And, of course, since that time, corporal punishment in school has become extremely rare. But unfortunately, much of what I'd later recall as the most damaging aspects of those years—including the ruthless competition and single-minded focus on content—persists in some form or other in many contemporary public and private schools.

Hour after hour, we had to sit with our hands folded in front of us, as we repeated our teacher's promptings. In first grade, we were obliged to memorize the Baltimore catechism, the English version of the Catholic dogma. In second grade, we learned the Latin phrases that accompanied the mass. By fourth grade, we were memorizing times tables, math formulas, historical dates, and grammar rules by parroting them back to our teachers.

Our desks were lined up in rows, with the students who performed best sitting in front and the struggling ones exiled to the back. Most students bought into the system and competed fiercely, for fear of ridicule both from their teachers and their classmates. We didn't expect, nor were we ever encouraged to believe, that a teacher would want to broaden our horizons, spark our creativity, or teach us self-awareness or empathy. We simply wanted to survive until the last bell rang and we were free.

I remember only a single time when I'd hoped for something more. I was six years old, and the youngest of six children, when I lost my father to cancer. On the day after his funeral, I raised my hand in class.

I held my hand in the air for what seemed like a very long time before the teacher called on me.

"I just want you to know that my daddy died—" I began.

"Yes, Thomas, we already know that," the nun said, and continued her lesson.

As I recall, I shrank back into my seat, feeling worse than invisible. As I would later learn, it wasn't as if the school didn't care about my family. The principal had already reached out to my mother and offered her a scholarship to keep her kids enrolled. Still, the message in the classroom was clear: emotions weren't allowed.

Is it any wonder that more than a decade later, I was so powerfully drawn to a philosophy supporting more compassionate understanding and behavior toward students?

Reading Jonathan Kozol's *Death at an Early Age* in college inspired me to set my sights on a teaching career. I'd eagerly take the paperback out of my back pocket to read during idle stretches while working at a flower stand in San Francisco, a job that helped pay my way through school. Kozol was the first author I'd read who seemed to describe an alternative to my own pedestrian education, and I longed for an equally heroic career. I still didn't know there was a name, not to mention a powerful history and research-based pedagogy, behind the alternative I was seeking.

I started graduate school in the mid-1970s during a new wave of enthusiasm for more informal, creative schools. These were the years of the "Open Classroom" movement. Now I think of this time as the second wave of the Progressive Education movement, as there were certainly echoes of progressive philosophy in the idea of a school without walls, in which children of all ages could roam, engaged in hands-on projects, guided by their interests, with teachers serving mostly as facilitators. Still, I can't recall my instructors explicitly relating any of this to the ground-breaking work of Dewey or Parker. At the time, the Open Classroom movement seemed more like an original product of the anti-authoritarian 1960s; and by the early 1980s, it had almost entirely vanished.

The Sputnik moment for the Open Classroom movement came in 1983, when a blue-ribbon commission appointed by Ronald Reagan's Secretary of Education, T. H. Bell, delivered a scathing report, entitled, *A Nation at Risk*, whose famously ominous conclusion warned that "the educational foundations of our society are presently being eroded by a rising tide of mediocrity that threatens our very future as a Nation and a people."

The response this time was a fervent and growing bipartisan campaign for more accountability from schools, mostly in the form of more of those standardized tests. And by 2001, "accountability" had become a buzzword. Under President George W. Bush that year, the "No Child Left Behind" Act tied federal funding to students' performance on tests. Eight years later, President Barack Obama's "Race to the Top" program sought similar results, although this time using carrots instead of sticks. However the federal policy was constructed, the message was becoming clear: for schools to survive, their students would have to score high on mandated tests. Teachers consequently understood that to preserve their own jobs, they'd have to spend more time and energy on memorization and drills. The classrooms of the so-called Third Industrial Revolution began to look ever more like the dreary common schools of the turn of the twentieth century, and the spirit of Emile retreated once again.

TRAVELS WITH TOM

While it may seem surprising that any explicitly progressive schools managed to survive through all this fear and federal policy, several dozen of them have endured. In the spring of 2013, I determined to visit a large sample, in order to investigate how century-old progressive values persist in today's schools, and to assess the chance that this valuable legacy might once again become a dominant influence in U.S. education.

Eight years earlier, I had joined half a dozen colleagues in reviving our national organization, which we've renamed the Progressive Education Network, or PEN. I served as its president from early 2011 to late 2013, during which time we've hosted four national conferences, each one larger and more optimistic than the last. We serve thousands of educators throughout America, and have filled hotel ballrooms in San Francisco, Washington D.C., Chicago, and Los Angeles with national experts, authors, and educators sharing news of best practices in designing curriculum, addressing learning differences, and understanding neuroscience advances.

The only area in which we've been consistently less than cutting edge is in protecting and promoting our brand—telling the world, clearly, who we are and what we do.

Again and again, I hear progressive educators struggling to clearly define what makes us different from conventional schools. This is actually an old story. There's a common joke that if you ask twenty of us to define Progressive Education, you'll get twenty-one different answers.

Lawrence Cremin, in his book about the first eight decades of the movement, went so far as to rule out any hope of a "capsule" definition of Progressive Education. "None exists, and none ever will," he wrote, "for throughout its history education meant different things to different people, and these differences were only compounded by the remarkable diversity of American education."

Despite my great respect for Cremin, I believe this is a disservice. It's not only possible to clearly define what we do—it is our moral imperative. Only by becoming better and more coherent advocates can we help move our highly effective strategies into the mainstream, where they belong.

This was my goal in February 2013, as I took a leave from my duties at Park Day to visit what ultimately would be forty-five progressive schools throughout America, interviewing teachers, students, parents, and principals. At the time, I didn't yet know of my illness, and felt blessed with abundant energy and time as I took planes, trains, and rental cars to journey between big cities, suburbs, and farmland. I conducted more than 100 hours of interviews, hoping to take up where Cremin had left off: to portray the state of Progressive Education in the years since the

1960s, and to capture the elusive prize of a concise definition of our craft.

I toured a mix of private and public schools, ranging from the racially diverse, inner-city Mission Hill, in Boston, to the mostly white, rural, private Putney School for high-schoolers in Vermont. I also visited several schools, which, like Park Day, engage in ambitious fund-raising and scholarship programs to serve students from a range of financial backgrounds. I chose the schools mainly for their reputations for excellence, including some that explicitly call themselves "progressive," such as the Wickliffe Elementary School, and others that unmistakably follow progressive practices but strategically avoid the "p-word," including Sidwell Friends School, the K–12 private school in Washington, D.C., where the Obamas, at this writing, send their daughters.

By my estimation, fewer than one hundred American schools still call themselves progressive. Many of the teachers and heads of these schools have confided to me that they feel isolated and adrift. "Tom, what is 'Progressive Education,' and are we still doing it?" I've been asked more than once.

Yet I also saw much evidence of the movement's hardy survival. Again and again, I found I could walk into a progressive classroom in New York City, inner-city Boston, or a suburb in Illinois or Ohio, and instantly feel at home. Children at these schools always seem to be somehow lighter, happier, and more engaged. Most of the time, kids are out of their chairs. There are similar inspirational mottos on the walls, and there's always a rug in the corner of the classrooms, where the younger students can learn in comfort and focus on strengthening their classroom community during part of the day.

When I've lingered to observe, I've also always noted the common pedagogy: the attention to relationships, the students' freedom, within limits, to follow their interests, and the hands-on, creative projects that reveal the deeper meanings behind the curricula. Given the steep decline in recent years in formal instruction in progressive strategies, this uniformity strikes me as remarkable.

At each school I visited, I asked teachers and principals to tell me how they defined Progressive Education, and as I listened to my tapes on my return, I found that while their words and emphasis varied considerably, they ended up here, too, having much in common.

Culling the similarities from hundreds of answers, I came up with my own capsule definition, clearer than any I have heard to date. It's this: *Progressive Education prepares students for active participation in a democratic society, in the context of a child-centered environment, and with an enduring commitment to social justice.*

I also found I could enumerate six core strategies, passed down from Dewey, Parker, and the other pioneers, and still in robust practice at progressive schools today. These are:

1. Attention to children's emotions as well as their intellects;
2. Reliance on students' interests to guide their learning;
3. Curtailment or outright bans on testing, grading, and ranking;
4. Involvement of students in real-world endeavors, ranging from going on field trips to managing a farm;
5. The study of topics in an integrated way, from a variety of different disciplines; and, not least,
6. Support for children to develop a sense of social justice and become active participants in America's democracy.

As I read this list, it seems vexingly abstract, even clinical. Yet when I think of these methods, vivid memories flood into my mind, forming a portrait of a pedagogy of joy.

In the hope of making our methods as vibrant to you as they are to me, I'll focus in the subsequent chapters on describing and explaining these six methods, as we continue our tour of Park Day School and go on to visit other schools that are living laboratories of our best national education traditions—a legacy we can't afford to keep secret any longer.

CHAPTER 2

The Rug
Teaching to the "Whole Child"

Saleh Khalaf, a nine-year-old Iraqi who was wounded in the U.S. invasion of his country, walks with new friends down a hall at Park Day School, where you could spend hours just reading the walls.   Photograph by *San Francisco Chronicle*

> *To the doctor, the child is a typhoid patient; to the playground supervisor, a first baseman; to the teacher, a learner of arithmetic. At times, he may be different things to each of these specialists, but too rarely is he a whole child to any of them.*
>
> —From the 1930 report of the White House
> Conference on Children and Youth

A MAGIC CARPET RIDE

A dozen six- and seven-year-olds sit and sprawl on the ten-by-ten-foot forest green rug in Susan Erb's first-grade classroom at Park Day School. Half of them manage to hold still, but the others are constantly moving. They rock back and forth, play with their hair, bump into each other, and, gasping with impatience, wave their hands to get Susan's attention.

On the floor between the students and the teacher lie two plastic hoops, each no bigger than a child's head. One is labeled "Needs" and the other "Wants." There is also a pile of blue index cards, each written with a single word or phrase, including: "Air," "Clean Water," "Clothes," "Dogs," "Toys," "House," and "Love." Taking turns, the students pick up cards and decide whether to put them in one hoop or the other.

Guided by Susan, whose cheerful charisma seems as fresh as it was on the day I first watched her teach nearly forty years ago, the students are learning about several things at once. Most obviously, they're figuring out the difference between needs and wants—with lively ancillary discussions about whether people always die from lack of shelter, how much easier it is for animals to bite you if you don't have clothes, and how many days someone can live without food. They're also learning about Venn diagrams, since by overlapping the hoops—thus creating a small, new space where cards may fit in both hoops at once—they can see how some needs are also wants, and vice versa.

Most important, however, these children are learning about attention, self-control, and empathy. For all their restlessness, they're already a strikingly well-behaved group of first-graders, instantly responsive to Susan's subtle coaching. They raise their hands instead of interrupting, and at least most of the time make obvious efforts to listen to each other.

Instead of calling out, they use silent hand signals: air quotes for "ditto" to show they agree, or air-slicing motions to show that they don't. A third signal, a thumb to a forehead, means "I need a brain break!"—a request for permission to go jump on the trampoline outside the door. Susan has signals of her own: she'll put a finger on her eyebrow, for instance, to silently encourage a child to "think!"

In a half-hour stretch, there is only one minor conflict, after one little girl hesitates to move aside to let another come back to her place after taking a turn.

When this happens, Susan stops the lesson immediately.

First, she reminds the class of their mantra: "If you see a problem, do something."

Then, she turns to the girl who has been blocked and who is now hugging her knees as if to make herself seem smaller.

"How did it feel when a friend didn't make a space for you?" Susan asks.

"Not good!" comes the muttered reply.

The offender, a pint-sized fashion plate in leggings and tunic top, glances at her classmate's face, taking in the impact of her behavior. She freezes, appearing to be in distress.

But Susan is ready with a remedy. "Shall we rewind and replay?" she suggests with a smile.

The entire group of children looks relieved; the offender grins and scoots aside, and the class promptly returns to a fervent debate about whether sharp arrows could pierce through a house and kill you, which may or may not mean the house is a need and not just a want. . . .

GETTING COMFORTABLE

In 1928, Mary Hammett Lewis, the founding headmistress of a different Park School—this one in Buffalo, New York—rhapsodized about the impact of a simple change to her classroom: the addition of a "big, friendly rug on which we might sit together for close companionship and comradely sharing of our interests."

She had hoped that the rug would reduce the formality of the "rigid chairs and desks," but it did much more than that. "It became a sort of magic carpet in my adventure," she wrote. "The attitude of the children changed completely the moment they set foot on the rug. Language lessons became confidential chats about all sorts of experiences. One day the rug became early Manhattan Island; another day it was the boat of Hendrick Hudson."

Although Lewis probably wasn't the first teacher to provide a classroom with a rug, she clearly conveyed why this cozy addition became a hallmark of progressive educators—the most vivid symbol of the idea that teachers are obliged to attend to students' emotional well-being if they wish to encourage their intellectual development. Everything we do stems from this notion of teaching to the "whole child," which, as I intend to show you, is as pragmatic in its impact on learning as it is compassionate.

In my travels to progressive schools throughout America, I found only a few classrooms (and mostly just for older students) that lacked a rug where students gathered daily. The tradition traces back to the ancient wisdom of Rousseau, Pestalozzi, and Froebel, who urged teachers to consider children's physical, moral, and spiritual needs—their bodies and hearts as well as their heads.

At Park Day School, most teachers start the morning with a meeting on the rug. It's here where the daily schedule is reviewed, where kids report on how they spent the weekend, and where many of our classes join in a morning meditation session. It's here, too, where students work out social problems that have come up at recess, where rules are reinforced, and where each new group starts to see itself as a mutually supportive team.

A comfortable classroom is key for the youngest students,

who are still getting used to leaving home each morning for the new daily routines of school. Yet comfort is also a powerful tool as students grow older: consider how the ease of a college seminar room, with sofas and coffee tables, may inspire entirely different behavior, and thinking, than a lecture hall, where students sit passively, taking notes. Like the rug, the seminar room tells students they can let their guard down. That leads to trust, which leads to strong relationships, which in turn can motivate risk-taking, creativity, and learning.

At Stanford's School of Business, Jonathan Berk, the former Park Day parent you met earlier, says he was inspired by watching children on our rugs to seek ways to help make his graduate students more comfortable as they study the art of critical thinking. "Most of us do not find it easy to have an open mind," Berk says. "That's really pretty much against human nature. So anything that helps students to relax physically can reduce that rigidity, making it easier to really listen to each other."

As Susan's virtuoso performance with her first-graders subtly shows, this is no simple task. Teachers' jobs would be much easier if they could limit themselves to making sure children were competently memorizing spelling, formulas, and historical dates. The best teachers strive to integrate those basics into an ongoing effort to build academically important skills, such as critical thinking and problem solving, while progressive educators are specially trained to also keep in mind group dynamics and each child's unique personality, developmental stage and progress, fears and anxieties, and social standing at the school.

The teachers mustn't overreach, particularly given that most have no formal therapeutic training. (Susan, a rare exception, began her career as an art therapist in a children's psychiatric hospital in New York City.) Yet neither should they ignore a century of best practices—nor, more importantly, the needs of their students. They understand they're obliged to bring their own hearts, as well as their heads, to their craft.

I don't mean to imply that conventional schools routinely disregard children's emotions. Many teachers, regardless of their schools' formal philosophies, will go out of their way to try to help kids cope with disputes on the playground and even problems at home. On a broader level, awareness of the potent link between cognitive and emotional development has dramatically increased over the past two decades, leading to considerably more teacher training in "social-emotional learning" (SEL) strategies to help students cultivate "emotional intelligence." Such awareness has grown considerably since the mid-1990s, when Daniel Goleman published his eponymous bestseller *Emotional Intelligence*, arguing that cognitive skills such as self-restraint and empathy can matter more than IQ in determining success and happiness. At present, forty-nine states have set standards for social-emotional learning programs for young children, while a bipartisan group of U.S. congressional representatives is seeking to increase SEL programming in public schools.

Even so, progressive educators are in a class by ourselves in having a century-long track record in teaching emotional intelligence. We're old hands at this, and have hundreds of thousands of emotionally skilled graduates to show for it.

STOP THE STRESS

Over the past century, ample research has helped justify the whole child approach at the core of progressive educators' practices.

Much of it boils down to a simple finding. Stress interferes with learning, diminishing focus and memory. Whether you're a soldier in Afghanistan or a second-grader, you are hard-wired to react to a perceived threat with the well-known "fight-or-flight" response, a phenomenon first documented in 1932 by the Harvard Medical School professor Walter Bradford Cannon. As part of this reaction, stress hormones flood the brain, shutting off non-emergency functions, including digestion, to help prepare the body for immediate action. In the short term, that can thwart high-level, nuanced thinking, learning, and memory. Repeated too often, it can cause long-lasting harm to the hippocampus, one of the brain's centers for learning and memory.

Now students, at least male students, need at least some stress to keep their eyes open and to focus. Two Progressive Era scientists, Robert Yerkes and John Dillingham Dodson, described this phenomenon in 1908, in what became a classic experiment. They found that giving rats mild electrical shocks would motivate them to run through a maze. Yet raising the intensity of the shocks past a certain level caused the rats to run around randomly as they helplessly tried to escape. The scientists drew a bell curve illustrating what came to be known as the Yerkes-Dodson law, conveying that there's an optimum level of stress needed for peak performance, after which focus and learning decline precipitously. (Interestingly, Tracey Shors and Amy Arnsten have shown that female rats and monkeys may do better without any stress at all. Adele Diamond's studies in humans may show this holds true to women of our species as well.)

Unfortunately, many children report feeling chronically overstressed and even threatened at school, whether it's from being teased or bullied, having to compete for test scores or grades, or being pressured by teachers who themselves are under pressure to raise their classes' test scores. This is particularly worrisome given that the impact of chronic stress is much more harmful to children, whose brains are still rapidly developing, than it is to adults, according to Stanford University neuroscientist Robert Sapolsky, a leading expert on stress who also happens to be a graduate of the John Dewey High School in Coney Island. "Everything I just told you about adult stress on the brain—multiply it ten-fold when you think about a ten-year-old's brain," Sapolsky has said.

It's sadly ironic that in our hopes for improving students' performance, particularly in math and science, we're setting many of them up for failure.

Sian Beilock, a University of Chicago psychology professor who spent her first three years of school at Park Day, gave me a striking example from her research. Beilock, the author of *Choke: What the Secrets of the Brain Reveal About Getting It Right When You Have To*, said many U.S. kindergartners today are already suffering from "math anxiety." "There's something to be said for lowering the pressure in those years," she noted. As a conscientious scientist, Beilock refrained from extrapolating from her own example, but she added that she was grateful for having spent her earliest school years in an atmosphere free of standardized tests.

CONNECTEDNESS IS KEY

More than a century ago, progressive educators clearly understood that when students aren't under excessive stress, they can be powerfully motivated by more positive emotions. For example, since learning is almost always a social pursuit, strong relationships with teachers and classmates can inspire students like little else.

For several years now, the federal Centers for Disease Control and Prevention (CDC) in Atlanta has been encouraging schools to improve students' sense of "connectedness," which the CDC defines as a belief that adults and other students at school care about them as individuals. The agency's research shows that a sense of connectedness improves students' grades and test scores as well as their lifelong health. At Park Day School, as at other progressive schools, we continually strive to create these healthy bonds by building communities where children feel valued and respected, and are considerate of each others' needs.

Plenty of additional evidence supports the benefits of this practice. Beginning in 1994, as part of the largest and most comprehensive long-term study of adolescents ever undertaken, federally funded researchers extensively and repeatedly interviewed more than 12,000 adolescents in grades 7 through 12, while also questioning their family members, fellow students, and school administrators. They found that students with strong relationships at school not only do better academically but are far less likely to drink too much, abuse drugs, skip school, bully other kids, and be sexually promiscuous. They're more likely to wear seat belts in cars, and less likely to carry weapons and have suicidal thoughts.

Stacey Wellman is a national authority on the power of strong relationships in school. Armed with no less than four master's degrees and up-to-date knowledge of research on brain science and learning, she's a full-time speech and language pathologist at the Winnetka Public School District in Illinois—America's only entire public school district that calls itself "progressive"—and a frequent lecturer to parents and educators. Wellman's bottom-line message is that children's academic as well as emotional development depends on strong relationships. That's why she recommends that teachers spend the first three weeks of each new academic year focusing on strengthening their class-room communities.

The advice makes even more sense if you recall the list of skills that employers say they're looking for these days, including creativity, critical thinking, and collaboration. All can be encouraged by an environment where it is safe to take intellectual risks. And the earlier the better: in Susan's first-grade class, a stuffed snake doll hangs from the ceiling with a legend saying, "In this classroom, it's okay to make missnakes," with the second "s" crossed out and replaced by a "t."

Wellman says she helps create such environments in the classes she teaches in part by knowing when some students, particularly the younger ones, are still too shy to raise their hands and participate in class discussions. Rather than cold-calling on them or trying to catch anyone off guard, she sometimes hands out paddles that students can write on with erasable pens, so that only she can see their comments or questions. "This is how I know immediately how many in the class are getting what I'm telling them," she says. With high school classes, Wellman sometimes lets students Tweet her. It's a much more collaborative model than that of most classrooms today, and one that also implies that a teacher can learn, in real time, whether his or her teaching is effective.

At Park Day School, we're constantly seeking a balance between the need to challenge children intellectually and the need to make sure that they feel emotionally safe. As Susan demonstrates with her first-graders on the rug, we encourage students to use language that reflects this intention. We teach them from the first day, for instance, to refer to each other as "friends." We don't expect they'll all become best buddies, but we do want to encourage an ethos of friendly behavior. That's why, when Susan confronted the failure of one of her first-graders to scoot aside for a classmate, she chose her words carefully, asking the aggrieved little girl, "How did it feel when a *friend* . . . ?"

On the first day of school, each Park Day kindergartner is assigned to a new friend from sixth grade. The older children show the younger ones around, eat lunch with them, and stay in close touch in subsequent weeks. Come the winter holidays, the sixth-graders, who have been steadily collecting interesting information on the new students, write fictional stories in which the kindergartners play starring roles. They then bind and decorate the books and present them to their young friends on the last day of school before the winter break.

Another way we help our students feel welcome is evident on our walls, which are virtual museums of children's artwork. You could easily spend several hours looking at the drawings and photographs, and reading the poetry and essays posted amid bulletins and class agreements.

Teachers' greetings and motivational mottos also take up a good deal of wall space. A sign on the middle school director's door promises visitors: "I will ask questions to try to understand you." Nearby, there's a chart with a list of brief details about every Park Day teacher—conveying a level of transparency that would have shocked the nuns at my old elementary school. The signs say: "I Bring Who I Am to Park Day School." Each of our staff members discloses his or her preferred name, ethnicity, fears, hopes, likes and dislikes. (One says she fears "injustice," while her "hidden talent" is making "delectable red velvet whoopee pies." Another confides her fear of her children moving far away "like I did to my parents in 1976.")

We're also big on blatant reminders that we expect our students to behave in ethical and emotionally healthy ways. A note on the sixth-grade humanities classroom vows: "I will take time to breathe deeply and I will remember to be grateful."

In 2003, the *San Francisco Chronicle* reported that our caring and focused community was "the ultimate medicine" for Saleh Khalaf, the nine-year-old boy who was maimed by a cluster bomb in Iraq. Khalaf attended Park Day School for a year on full scholarship while he endured multiple surgeries to remove shrapnel in his body and brain. Weeks before he arrived, many of our students had already made his acquaintance, writing get-well cards to him in the hospital after seeing him on TV. Once he got here, they were so solicitous that Khalaf made close friends long before he had a basic command of English. Dictating in Arabic to an interpreter, who translated for the rest of his classmates, Khalaf described how he used to catch fish in the river that ran by his house back home, and how he'd see hyenas and wild pigs at night. Last I checked, Khalaf and his father had permanently settled in California, and he had gone on to high school. Every student he met at Park Day School was enriched by our year of getting to know him.

LETTING KIDS BE KIDS

The conservative English philosopher Michael Oakeshott, who was born at the turn of the twentieth century and attended a progressive elementary school, wrote that "good schools bestow upon their graduates a recollection of childhood as a golden satisfaction . . . not as a passage of time hurried through on the way to more profitable engagements, but, with gratitude, as an enjoyed initiation into the mysteries of the human condition." These words may sound awfully quaint today, as our society's demands ramp up the pressure on children as soon as they leave kindergarten. Among these are increasingly competitive environments—a topic I'll explore in depth in chapter 3—and increasingly crowded classrooms, which I'll tell you about right here.

We've known for years that smaller student-teacher ratios help children in a variety of powerful ways. As educators, we see that smaller classes make young children feel safer and provide them with more nurturing attention. But these benefits were also borne out in a landmark study launched in Tennessee in 1989, involving 6,500 students in 339 schools, which concluded that smaller classes contribute to better relationships between students and teachers, fewer discipline problems, higher student motivation, better academic performance, fewer high school dropouts, and better teacher morale. They even lead to better long-term health for students, on average, since high school graduates tend to live healthier lives than their counterparts. Yet despite the strong evidence in their favor, as a rule, smaller student-teacher ratios unfortunately remain mostly a privilege of well-funded private schools, with class sizes for the vast majority of public school students fluctuating in parallel with economic booms and busts.

Beginning in the 1970s, many U.S. states responded to researchers' findings and invested in reducing the ratios. By 2009, the latest year for which figures are available, the public elementary school student-teacher ratio had fallen to 15.5, compared to 12.1 for private schools. (A caveat is that this federal statistic covers all certified school staff, including special education teachers, meaning that actual classroom ratios will be higher.)

Since June 2009, however, in the wake of the Great Recession, more than 300,000 teachers nationwide have lost their jobs, increasing the student-teacher ratio by 4.6 percent, according to a 2012 White House report. The report predicted the trend would worsen even more, and from what I've heard, it has.

Park Day School is an exception to this rule. We have managed to maintain an average student-teacher ratio of 11 to 1. We cap class size in K–3 grades at sixteen, while for older students, the class size never exceeds twenty students. This, we know, is a privilege of many private schools: our high tuition rates allow us to hire more teachers to keep class sizes down. (The fee for parents paying the full cost at Park Day ranges from $20,000 to $22,000 a year.) That's why I've been so impressed to learn of some progressive public schools that make smaller student-teacher ratios a priority even when it means sacrificing on other fronts. "When we develop our budget, we start with the child at the center," says Ayla Gavins, the widely respected head of the Mission Hill School, a small, pilot pre-K–8 public school in inner-city Boston. "We ask ourselves, what do our kids need most? And then we go from there." Mission Hill has no assistant principal or full-time PE teacher, but limits its class sizes to eighteen students at most.

Maintaining low student-teacher ratios is particularly important given all we've learned from neuroscience breakthroughs in recent years about the enormous variability in the way students learn. This encompasses not only the most extreme learning differences, including children on the ADHD and autism spectrums, but comparatively run-of-the-mill variations in children who learn at different speeds, regardless of their ages, and in different ways—for example, depending on whether information is presented through words or pictures.

It takes a lot of extra attention from teachers to understand how each child learns best and to individualize curriculum at least to some extent. Park Day School's reputation of being able to personalize teaching methods helps explain why nearly 30 percent of our students have some documented learning or behavioral challenge—more than twice the national average. In many cases, these children are enrolled by parents who are making considerable financial sacrifices to find a safe place for their kids to learn.

As head of school, I've made it a point to be aware not only of children's documented learning challenges but of the more routine developmental progress of each of our students—sometimes to the surprise of their parents.

About a decade ago, Michael Pollan, a writer, and his wife Judith Belzer, a painter, enrolled their son Isaac in our fifth-grade class, after the family moved to California from Connecticut. Part of Isaac's work over the next couple of years was to adjust to the unfamiliar west coast culture. He came armed with an east coast sarcasm, which by sixth grade had contributed to a clash with his Spanish teacher. I invited Pollan and Belzer to my office.

As Pollan would later remind me, they had expected me to come down hard on their son, and thus were taken aback when I began the meeting by assuring them that Isaac was "doing exactly what he was supposed to be doing," considering his age and circumstances. He was naturally inclined to rebel at that age, and his Spanish class was a safe place in which to do it. That didn't mean his behavior was appropriate or that he didn't need to make amends. We made sure he apologized to his teacher. But I wanted his parents to know that our policy at Park Day is not to turn children into villains.

F. Scott Fitzgerald famously wrote that "the test of a first-rate intelligence is the ability to hold two opposed ideas in the mind at the same time, and still retain the ability to function." This is our ambition, as progressive teachers, since we must continually weigh the needs of the institution—including teachers' needs to manage classrooms—with those of the child.

"A big part of what kids learn in school is how to become cogs in a bureaucracy," Isaac's father, Michael Pollan, recently told me. "If you're trying to do something more interesting and complicated than that, it's much harder."

Naturally not all teachers are on board with the degree of consideration for the needs of the child that we practice at Park Day. It's a value that requires a lot more communication between teachers, parents, and the head of the school, so that everyone's feelings are understood and respected. Over the past twenty-eight years, I've spent countless hours in long, involved meetings, considering multiple points of view, communicating, compromising, and ultimately, when we get it right, collaborating for the good of every child.

I'll confess I've had a secret that has helped me get through it. For most of my time at Park Day School, I've moonlighted, weekends and evenings, as a high school and college basketball referee. The job was a perfect counterpoint to my Mister Rogers role at the school. A referee never needs to seek consensus. He blows his whistle, and that's it.

You might chalk up my enthusiasm for this blessed release into a world of black and white and snap decisions as a part of my own "whole child."

CHAPTER 3

The Inner Ear
Learning That Ignites Children's Senses

A cardboard head, designed and constructed by elementary schoolchildren studying sensory abilities and disabilities at The Children's School in Berwyn, Illinois.
Photograph by Angela Whitacre de Resendiz

Education . . . is a process of living and not a preparation for future living. —JOHN DEWEY, *My Pedagogic Creed*, 1897

SENSING EMPATHY

Four eight-year-old girls take their places in front of a giant cardboard head and launch into breathy descriptions of the role of the inner ear in the proprioception system, by which people orient their bodies in space. One sticks her hand inside the head to point out a coil of plastic tubes and papier-mâché, representing the ear drum and cochlea. Another declares: "If you bump into someone, it doesn't mean you're clumsy—it's a proprioceptive error!"

Their teacher, Angela Whitacre de Resendiz, grins to hear one of the slogans her class has adopted during a spontaneous, two-month project on the senses at The Children's School, outside of Chicago.

Before the unit began, Whitacre herself hadn't heard of the proprioception system. But she noticed that several of her students had grown curious about why some of their classmates were often bumping into tables. They also wanted to know why some of them, but not others, were being allowed to sit on special beanbag chairs each day. Their questions led them first to research in the library and on the Internet, where they learned about how some people are born with sensory impairments that affect coordination and sensitivity to touch, sound, and light. Next, they took a field trip to the local playroom of a sensory-integration therapist. Parents contributed articles, and students filled out surveys that asked about their senses—including what kinds of stimuli make them feel overwhelmed, and how they cope. By the time they started to design and build the cardboard head, even Whitacre's husband, at home at night, was asking her questions about sensory issues.

The students were excited to learn that, in fact, people had more than five senses—that, as they chanted in another class slogan, it was more like "Twelve, and counting!" These included the sense of one's body moving through space, plus the somewhat related experience of balance. The sense of taste, meanwhile, could be distinguished as four separate senses, to register sweet, bitter, salty, or sour. The sense of touch could similarly be distinguished as sensations of heat and pressure. And the list went on, with each student gradually learning to appreciate how he or she fit along a spectrum of sensory strengths and weaknesses.

Through this personalized approach, the students explored cognitively advanced concepts with rare gusto, while also reaping some non-cognitive rewards. Children who had previously worried about being labeled as awkward became more relaxed. The class now understood that when kids asked to hold beanbags on their laps, it meant they were having a rough day. A new appreciation of how movement, noise, and visual clutter affected all of their abilities to focus led to class discussions of how to improve their collective study habits. And the entire class found new meaning in yet another slogan in long use at the school, namely: "Everybody's working on something."

LIFE LESSONS

I was delighted to come across The Children's School's inner-ear project during my travels to progressive schools in the Midwest. This single study unit perfectly embodied three of Progressive Education's hallmark teaching strategies, each developed more than a century ago, and all of which remain strikingly effective today, as demonstrated by published research. While each, to varying degrees, may also be found in modern conventional schools, I'm sure they could be benefiting additional millions of American students.

The historical names of these three methods are a mouthful: "emergent curriculum," "integrated curriculum," and "experiential education." In practice, however, they're easy to understand. I'll briefly explain each of them, and also show them in action.

The first one, "emergent curriculum," refers to teaching that responds to children's enthusiasms, as Whitacre did when she spontaneously embarked on a unit on the senses. These days you'll likely hear of this style of teaching referred to by other names, including "inquiry-based learning," but the rationale is similar: Students are most motivated to learn when they're already interested in something.

"Integrated curriculum" is the practice of approaching children's learning thematically, rather than compartmentalizing subjects such as math, English, and science. Thus, Whitacre's students learned science—human physiology—by studying the workings of the inner ear, while also practicing math concepts by designing their proportionally accurate model sensory system, and honing their writing skills by producing essays about their project. In this way, each discipline became more relevant than if they had studied it in isolation.

"Experiential education"—commonly referred to today as "project-based learning"—is just what it sounds like: learning by *doing*. Rather than goad students to bury their noses in their textbooks, teachers get them out of their chairs, using their hands, and working with others on a goal-oriented mission, such as building that giant cardboard head.

Uniting all three of Progressive Education's core strategies is the basic idea, so explicitly championed by John Dewey and his fellow educational reformers, that for school to be more meaningful, motivating, and effective, it needs to be more like real life. Children are naturally driven to imitate adults, Dewey pointed out, and the more their studies can connect with real-world, relevant adult activities, the more eager they are to pursue them.

Sound reasonable? Well, think back to what an enormous

contrast this worldview represents with the dreary schools described around the same time by the muckraker Joseph Rice. In one New York classroom Rice visited, students were forbidden even to move their heads during class. "Why should they look behind when the teacher is in front of them?" their principal reasoned.

Progressive reformers understood that such harsh restraint could kill children's natural love of learning. So instead they freed students from their desks, while transforming their classrooms by adding musical instruments, hammers and saws, and theater costumes. Their modern heirs continue to value raw experience at schools such as the Burgundy Farm Country Day School, in Alexandria, Virginia, a private, pre-K–8 school set on twenty-five partially wooded acres. Burgundy students camp out twice a year in a nearby cove for immersion learning about science and wildlife, while at the William T. Sherman School, PS 87, a public K–5 school on the Upper West Side of Manhattan, first-graders create a restaurant in their classroom, organizing menus, preparing food, and serving meals for their parents.

EMERGENT CURRICULUM—FOLLOW THAT CHILD!

Deborah Meier would have made John Dewey proud. In 1987, she was the first educator to win a MacArthur "genius award," celebrating her work as founder of a network of small, progressive, and successful public schools for disadvantaged students in East Harlem, New York. At eighty-two years old, she has spent the past half century as a teacher, principal, author, blogger, and public speaker, and she continues to follow a travel schedule matching the pace of her lively imagination.

Meier often talks about how skilled teachers constantly pivot to follow a child's curiosity. Several years ago, she told me, she had taken a small group of kindergartners on an outing to New York's Central Park, when she found herself spending an hour in a fervent debate about whether rocks were alive. The group had been following a curriculum guide suggesting that kids distinguish between living and non-living things that they find in natural settings. One little boy refused to agree with Meier's gentle suggestion that a rock he picked up should go in the cardboard box she carried that was marked "non-living."

"He reminded me that I had said just the week before that the rocks in Central Park had come from glaciers all the way from the North Pole to settle here," Meier explained, conceding that her choice of words might have been a bit misleading.

The boy went on to hypothesize that the rocks have "babies," since they break into littler rocks, and soon had managed to persuade other children to his line of thinking, to the point that Meier felt obliged to put aside her plans for the rest of the afternoon so as to calmly continue the discussion. "Young people need to have their ideas taken seriously," she said. "They have their ideas, and we often think they're just cute, and try to correct them. But democracy rests on people taking each other's ideas seriously and having the confidence to look for evidence to support them. We should start them early in this: it's a core preparation for being a good and well-educated citizen."

This style of education is also more in tune with the way humans are wired to learn, say evolutionary psychologists including Peter Gray, a research professor at Boston College, and the author of *Free to Learn: Why Unleashing the Instinct to Play Will Make Our Children Happier, More Self-Reliant, and Better Students for Life*. Gray argues that young children have an innate drive to learn, which is often stifled by imposed curriculum. "We're teaching the child that his questions don't matter, that what matters are the questions of the curriculum. That's just not the way natural selection designed us to learn. It designed us to solve problems and figure things out that are part of our real lives," Gray has said.

Meier so diligently practiced what she preached that she ended up calling an acquaintance, a biochemist at Rockefeller University, to ask his take on the living-rocks debate. While he ultimately agreed with Meier's view that the rocks weren't actually living, he acknowledged that at least some differences might indeed be subtle, and admired the students' line of reasoning. "Tell your students," he urged her, "that they're on the cutting edge of modern science."

The idea that children aren't born as blank slates to be filled in by wise adult knowledge but rather arrive on Earth with preexisting drives and ready-to-be developed curiosity, which their educators would do well to respect, carries familiar echoes from Rousseau's *Emile*. You might say it goes back even further, to when Socrates noted that "Wonder is the beginning of wisdom." Yet it seems to be a lesson we need to learn over and over again. "The model of the child as an empty vessel to be filled with knowledge provided by the teacher must be replaced," declared a landmark 2000 National Research Council report, *How People Learn: Brain, Mind, Experience, and School.*

In fact, the very first of three key findings elaborated in that seminal report was that students come to school with preconceptions about the world, and that "If their initial understanding is not engaged, they may fail to grasp the new concepts and information that are taught, or they may learn them for the purposes of a test but revert to their preconceptions outside the classroom." Thus, urged the authors, "the teacher must actively inquire into students' thinking, creating classroom tasks and conditions under which student thinking can be revealed."

This has always been one of our top goals at Park Day—indeed, it's been that way for more than thirty-seven years—which is just one reason why I'm continually bemused to hear such approaches hailed as pioneering. "How a Radical New Teaching Method Could Unleash a Generation of Geniuses," read a recent headline in *Wired* magazine, for a story extolling the rightfully acclaimed educational researcher and TED Talk 2013 winner Sugata Mitra, who had the purportedly revolutionary idea of turning a group of ten-to-fourteen-year-olds loose to study science on their own. The author enthused that "a new breed of educators . . . are inventing radical new ways for children to learn, grow, and thrive. To them, knowledge isn't a commodity that's delivered from teacher to student but something that emerges from the students' own curiosity-fueled exploration. Teachers provide prompts, not answers, and then they step aside so students can teach themselves and one another."

The article omitted the fact that progressive educators figured out the merits of this teaching approach more than a century ago. But at least it recognized the kind of education we need to meet the demands of today's economy. It seems so obvious: If we truly want to encourage our kids to be critical thinkers, problem solvers, and collaborators, we have to give them opportunities to practice those skills early on. And if we hope to spur innovation to keep our economy humming, we must find ways to free students to pursue some of their wildest ideas.

The founders of the Progressive Education Association thought well and hard about how to accomplish these ends before their inaugural April 1919 meeting in Washington, D.C. The band of school founders and freelance reformers included Marietta Johnson, the future author Stanwood Cobb, and Anne E. George, directress of the Washington Montessori School and an admirer of John Dewey's brand of Progressive Education. By that time, they had been turning the tables on conventional schools for several years, giving children unprecedented freedom to pursue their interests, to learn at their own paces, and to explore their world through free time and play—and they knew their techniques were working. The most important of their founding principles was that students should be free from "arbitrary laws," with permission for "initiative and self-expression"; that "interest" should motivate all of their work; and that the teacher would be a "guide" as opposed to a "task-master."

These three principles capture the soul of the progressive reform movement, and what made and still makes it so different from mainstream approaches. They're also proof that progressive educators came up with many of today's "radical new teaching methods" back in the age of the Model T.

SPEAKING OF SPONTANEITY: FAIR PLAY

You might consider play as the purest example of children following their interests—and, largely for that reason, play has become a hot topic in education circles in recent years. Educators have been fretting over the shrinking role of play, not just during the school day but in children's lives in general.

Neuroscientists contend that for adults and children alike, play is a ramp to joyful learning: an exercise with the power to bolster social and cognitive skills, improving problem solving, creativity, abstract thinking, and collaboration. We limit opportunities for play at our peril, they warn. Alison Gopnik, a psychology professor at the University of California at Berkeley and co-author of books including *The Scientist in the Crib*, suggests that diminishing time for play can make children less adaptable. When computer scientists build robots, Gopnik notes, they purposefully don't program every move because in this way, the robots become more flexible, virtually learning from their mistakes.

On my travels to progressive schools, I spoke with many educators who are so concerned about the reduction of spontaneity in children's lives that they are literally trying to institutionalize play, ironic as that may seem. At my own school, Park Day, Susan Erb began declaring "mandatory block-building days" in her first-grade class after she noticed several years ago, to her dismay, that many of the younger kids had never played with blocks, and initially seemed at a loss of what to do with them. "At first, they just wanted to create narratives from their electronic games," she says. Like many teachers I know, Susan fears that increasingly pervasive electronics are eroding children's spontaneity and focus. She sees a more relaxed form of play as an antidote, as well as an opportunity to train little hands and imaginations.

In a similar spirit, at the Common School in Amherst, Massachusetts, students begin each day with an hour of free-choice time, which they refer to as "winging." During this hour, they may choose to work or play, but either way, they're practicing the skill of structuring their time. Free to visit any classroom in the school, some fifth-graders visit their first-grade "buddies" to read to them on the classroom rug, while others may work on a project in the art room. Teachers may use this time to confer with their colleagues or meet with students who need extra help with a skill or concept. The "winging" hour is a hallmark of the school, which has an extraordinarily close community and relaxed atmosphere.

Together with other heads of schools, I often find myself citing the pragmatic benefits of play to parents who worry that their children might be having too much fun at school. Frankly, I worry they're not having *enough* fun. It is vastly easier to produce adults who are lifelong learners if they've learned to enjoy learning as kids.

Along these same lines, art and music education, with all the opportunities they offer for joy and spontaneity, are powerful ways to entice children to learn. More is the pity that so many public schools have been drastically cutting back on these opportunities. The last ten years have brought a double whammy: not only has the push for higher test scores limited time spent on anything other than rote academics, but increasingly severe state budget cuts that were underway even before the Great Recession have resulted in layoffs of art and music teachers. Not surprisingly, the cutbacks have dealt the sharpest blows to the most vulnerable schools. While families in wealthier districts often raise and donate money to save their art and music programs, low-income, urban schools usually lack this Plan B.

In 2013, the national Center on Budget and Policy Priorities found that schools serving more than 95 percent of American youth had cut funding since the recession, and that as a result, most schools serving children from low-income families had reduced or abolished their art and music programs. Making matters worse, researchers have found that it is just these students who stand to benefit most from art and music classes at school, not least because their families lack the resources of wealthier classmates, who can fund them on their own. One National Endowment study found that low-income high school students who earned few or no arts credits were five times more likely to drop out of high school than low-income students who earned many arts credits. Other research has found that arts can be a powerful motivator for otherwise disengaged students to stay in school, drawing on hidden talents, building confidence, and providing social support. Apparently, arts education can even improve test scores. One study found that students who took four years of art and music classes in high school scored 91 points higher on their SATs than students who took half a year of art or less.

Art and music education were virtually unknown in American schools before progressive educators challenged the drab status quo. But the early reformers worked to make culture a major part of students' lives, a practice that continues, exuberantly, today. To walk into a progressive school is to be immediately surrounded by the arts—from vivid murals and life-sized papier-mâché sculptures to hip-hop dance shows to classical music recitals and ballet. A hallmark of our schools is that children's artwork is hung throughout every public space—and even floats from lighting fixtures and rafters. Teachers take every opportunity to get students drawing and painting, writing poetry, building models, and composing music to accompany their academic projects.

This artistic abundance is by no means an exclusive perk of our wealthiest private schools. At Mission Hill, the Boston public school, for instance, clear priorities and smart budget management have helped preserve a full-time music teacher who coordinates instrumental and vocal programs for every student. At the Odyssey public charter school in Pasadena, the faculty aggressively seeks grants and donations and recruits parent volunteers to make sure children participate in hands-on opportunities with visiting artists and field trips to museums and concerts.

INTEGRATED CURRICULUM: CONNECT THE DOTS

In their quest to make school more relevant and engaging, progressive educators argued that students should no longer study subjects in isolation, with an hour for math followed by an hour for English, followed by an hour for science, and so on. When the journalist-pediatrician Joseph Rice toured progressive schools in the early 1900s, he was struck by the way teachers were experimenting with presenting material thematically—a technique, he reflected, that endowed each subject with more meaning as it could be seen in its relation with another.

Interdisciplinary learning is fundamental to making school more like life. As Maureen Cheever, my friend and fellow board member of the Progressive Education Network, says, "When I go for a walk, it's not like I'm thinking, 'I'm just going to think about math for the next forty minutes.' " Once again, however, modern researchers have gone to the trouble of extensively confirming the value of the interdisciplinary approach that progressive teachers have followed for so many decades. In fact, the second of the three top findings in the National Research Council report *How People Learn* cited students' need to "understand facts and ideas in the context of a conceptual framework." This, wrote the scientists, helps them learn information more quickly and transfer what they've learned to new situations.

More than thirty years ago, during my own teaching career at Park Day, I routinely planned my classes by drawing a web. I'd put the topic to be studied—say, the circulatory system—in the middle, and draw lines out to different disciplines, such as science, math, English, and the arts. We've gotten a lot more sophisticated about this at Park Day School in the years since then, and today we have established lesson plans, well tested over time, which entice children into studying subjects from several points of view.

In fifth grade, for instance, students study watersheds as members of small research groups that explore general questions such as "How are creeks formed?" using their science, math, and writing skills. The groups take a series of field trips out to a nearby creek, where they periodically measure water levels and calculate flow rates. Then they write blogs and prepare audiovisual presentations on what they've learned.

A more elaborate example is Joan Wright-Albertini's annual ecosystem unit for her first-graders. Each year, this ingenious teacher turns her classroom into a scene from a desert, rain forest, or moonscape, depending on the children's interests at the time.

Shortly after the 2010 oil spill in the Gulf of Mexico, for instance, Joan's students chose to create an underwater forest, with glistening fish made of aluminum foil and a huge papier-mâché octopus with streaming paper legs. The students studied the biology of the sea animals, wrote essays about them, and then dressed up in goggles and homemade cardboard air tanks to introduce other classes and groups of parents to their wonderland. That year, however, as Joan has done for the past fifteen years of teaching this unit, she delivered a surprise. On the morning after the students served as proud docents to their classroom, they arrived to find yellow tape, marked CAUTION, blocking their entrance, and giant black lawn bags crumpled on the floor. "There's been an oil spill!" their teacher told them, before leading them to another classroom. There, she showed the students videos of oil spills, acquainting them with how such a disaster would affect each of the fish, birds, and animals they had so carefully constructed. The experience "broke my heart in two," one little girl said. But Joan didn't let things rest there. "It's a little controversial to do this with first-graders—it's such an emotional hit for them," she acknowledged. "That's why the next step is so important. They need to know there's something they can do." The children donned gardening gloves and simulated haz-mat suits and energetically "cleaned up" their classroom. As Joan recalled, they had come to think of the ocean as "theirs" and were eager to protect it.

Some progressive schools carry the thematic learning concept to truly impressive extremes. At the Children's Community School in Van Nuys, California, fifth- and sixth-graders begin studying island cultures by "inventing" an island, which they proceed to describe in terms of geology, geography, resources, and demographics. With the help of the art teacher, they build three-dimensional maps of their island, to scale, on large pieces of plywood. They also write and illustrate history books about their island, which they illustrate with linoleum block prints. Next, they study Hawaiian culture, during which they learn about everything from native mythology and foods to how to dance the hula and play the ukulele. The unit culminates with a five-day field trip to Hawaii, during which the students, who have assiduously raised funds for months in advance to pay all their travel expenses, study geology, ecology, and culture, and tour a beach to see a program that is trying to help preserve sea turtles.

MAKE IT REAL

When it comes to making school more like life, there's nothing to compare with giving students real-life jobs. That's the operating plan at the Putney School, a private boarding school set on 500 acres near the town of Brattleboro, Vermont, where high school students operate a dairy farm. The students are responsible for all of the work on the farm, including caring for thirty dairy cows, tending to the vegetable crops, and selling excess produce in local markets. Carmelita Hinton, who founded the school in 1935, envisioned an institution that would be a "more real, less self-centered venture," and so it remains today. At Putney, students are constantly using their hands, whether they're applying antibiotic cream to a calf's infected udder, harvesting broccoli, or throwing clay on a potter's wheel. The faculty expects them to behave like responsible young adults, juggling work obligations with demanding academic and arts classes. If they fail to complete their assigned farm chores, they can be disciplined and even expelled.

The Putney School farm is a dramatic showcase of what twentieth-century progressive reformers referred to as "experiential education" and twenty-first-century education buffs call "project-based learning." One of the earliest advocates of this strategy was William Heard Kilpatrick, a Teachers College professor at Columbia University, and the author of *The Project Method* (1918). Kilpatrick had been inspired by the work of Dewey and of Edward Thorndike, a prominent researcher of human motivation and learning. He contended, in what was then a novel idea, that students might need motivation—other than fear—to learn well.

When it came to putting their theories into practice, however, few of the early reformers were more inventive than the Winnetka school superintendent Carleton Washburne, who was known by friends as "Jelly Legs" for his unusually long limbs. Washburne taught first-graders about the postal system by creating a school post office, and had fourth-graders learn about astronomy by viewing the night sky through a telescope and building a solar system to scale in the school gymnasium. He also organized "student corporations" that offered hands-on experience with working-world pursuits. Kids bred chickens, rabbits, and hamsters to sell, worked in the school cafeteria in exchange for free lunch, and even made loans through a student credit union.

In modern times, project-based learning (PBL) remains one of the most influential and enduring gifts of progressive educators. Abundant research validates its power to increase motivation and help students retain what they've learned. One widely cited study of two British secondary schools, for instance, comparing one that used projects and another that stuck to lectures, found striking differences in understanding and achievement among students who were tested on math problems requiring analytical skills. Three times as many students at the project-based school achieved the top grade on the national math examination. Other researchers have found that well-designed projects tackling real-world problems help develop those much-touted twenty-first-century skills of communication, collaboration, critical thinking, and creativity—so much so that some educators say project-based learning will be key to helping students adapt to and excel under the new Common Core state standards.

The benefits of educational projects have in fact been so widely recognized by now that it's rare to find a conventional school that hasn't tried to incorporate them in some way. Still, in many cases, sadly, that means nothing more imaginative than busywork involving team reports illustrated with dioramas or other visual aids.

Progressive schools aim higher. At the Miquon School, a private elementary school in Conshohocken, Pennsylvania, founded by parents in 1932, a recent project assigned kindergartners as custodians of a new goldfish pond. The children were naturally drawn to both the sensory pleasures of the pond—the coolness

of the water on their hands and the bright flickers of the fish—
and the challenge of keeping their wards alive. Questions arose
easily, such as how the fish breathed when the pond was covered
with ice, and how often the fish needed to be fed in different sea-
sons. The children came up with a list of rules, including that
they would keep the pond clean, avoid throwing anything in it,
and refrain from stepping on the plants around it. During winter, their list included the injunctions: "Don't tap on the ice or
the fish can be dead," and "Make sure there are air holes so the
fish can have fresh air." By the end of the project, the children
had an intuitive understanding of ecosystems and conservation
that would likely last a lifetime.

At Park Day School, our projects are always closely related to
units of study. Our first-graders routinely complete a multi-
week unit on bridges, including field trips to observe and report
on Bay Area bridges and a stop at Oakland Technical High
School's engineering school to discuss the bridge-building
competition that goes on there. The unit culminates with students designing and building their own bridges with materials
running the gamut from sugar cubes to cardboard to pipe
cleaners, all the way up to one class project that built a bridge
between four trees on campus, using woven recycled fire hose.
The project tests students' mastery of newly learned concepts
from physics and engineering, such as compression and tension
and live and dead loads.

The most successful student projects include a "framing
question" or goal, which gives students a strong sense of purpose. At Park Day, fifth-graders studying the relationship
between early American settlers and native Algonquin Nation
residents on Roanoke Island off the banks of North Carolina.
Teachers Lesley Bell and Alex Kane encourage the students to
imagine how they might have handled conflict between the two

groups, if they had been in charge on one side or the other. The students immerse themselves in the compelling story, reading history, learning the crafts of the time, and acting out skits in which they play the roles of settlers and Native Americans.

The project-based approach to learning can often motivate even the most alienated students. Stacey Wellman, the Winnetka School District's learning specialist, tells the story of a high school student who was utterly uninterested in reading *The Great Gatsby* and in danger of failing English until her teacher allowed her to approach the book by designing clothes the characters might wear. Her score shot up as soon as she discovered a reason to care about F. Scott Fitzgerald's novel for reasons other than fearing a bad grade on a test.

Putting students in charge of serious-minded projects—whether caring for cows or goldfish or trying to figure out why early American settlers ended up fighting with natives—has great psychological power, not least because it conveys that adults have high expectations of them. As researchers have found, this can often be a self-fulfilling prophecy. In a classic study of the so-called Pygmalion effect, in 1964, a psychologist named Robert Rosenthal told elementary schoolteachers that intelligence tests had indicated that some of the students, who were in fact chosen at random, were poised to bloom intellectually that year, while others wouldn't. The teachers were so influenced by this prediction that their treatment of the students changed over time, and, lo and behold, the students who had been identified as ready to bloom added more points to their IQ scores than their classmates.

Similarly, students from the Putney School, who are trusted to an extraordinary degree to behave responsibly by taking care of valuable livestock, almost invariably succeed. Emily Jones, the Putney head of school, told me that one of the biggest challenges these kids have is when they go off to college and feel alienated from less independent and resilient classmates.

NO EASY DAY

If I had a nickel for every time I've heard or read Progressive Education called "permissive," "fluffy," or "loosey-goosey," I could buy that first-edition copy of Lawrence Cremin's history of the movement that I've had my eye on for the past twenty years. People who make these charges simply don't get it. Teaching in the authentic progressive tradition, with the extremely high standards set by Dewey and his followers, demands much more of students and their teachers than does conventional methods.

Rather than relying on a text and repeating a successful unit of study, year after year, as so many teachers do, progressive educators—like Whitacre, with her unit on the inner ear—must listen carefully and patiently until they recognize the genuine interests of their students, and then be ready to turn on a dime. They build units from scratch and adapt them as they go, pivoting according to the interests, strengths, and challenges of their students. I found it disappointing, but not surprising, that even some of the progressive schools I visited had abandoned this practice of responsiveness to children's interests beyond the third or fourth grades, such is the pressure to cover a mandated curriculum. Schools in general are becoming a lot more risk-averse, and this spontaneous approach indeed can risk some unproductive detours. On balance, however, it can encourage children's love of learning for the rest of their lives, which I'd say is a risk well worth taking. The trick is to skillfully combine spontaneity and interest with conveying the basics of our common culture, empowering children to have confidence in their command of math, English, history, and science. On my visits to the forty-five progressive schools, I was continually in awe of how teachers were managing to carry it off.

Whitacre transferred to the Children's School from a more conventional setting, and acknowledged that her first year at the progressive school was "very scary. I went from having a really strict curriculum that I could secretly bend and twist when the door was closed to having the door open but no written formula for what I needed to cover: no Tuesday you need to study vocabulary words, or anything like that. At my old school, at the end of the day, if the students didn't learn the five things they were supposed to learn, the responsibility was on them, but here, it's on me. It's also more like I need to figure out who they are, versus that they need to follow instructions."

Whitacre acknowledged that Progressive Education was certainly more challenging but also "a lot more fun. Since I've started teaching here, I build stuff at my house, and my kids build stuff, and I draw things. I have a curiosity about the world that has been rekindled. I get e-mails all the time from parents suggesting projects—maybe something they heard on the radio—and my whole family gets excited. You get caught up in it, and it's contagious. Maybe it sounds cheesy. But my husband now knows more about proprioception than I do."

The Magic Circle
Building Character and Community

Eighth-grade students working on the literary journal at the Cambridge Friends School in Massachusetts.   Photograph by Gila Lyons

> *The primary concern of education is character. A school should be a model home, a complete community, an embryonic democracy.*
>
> —COLONEL FRANCIS W. PARKER

THE BUDDY SYSTEM

As an eighth-grader at the Cambridge Friends School in Massachusetts, Sam Rueter, an amateur poet and basketball player, got a chance to try his hand as an editor of a new literary journal. In a collaborative project, Rueter's English class embarked on producing a single-issue magazine that they named This Is Not a Drill. *Their teacher told them that the students would be responsible for editing and serving on planning committees, as well as submitting work. She encouraged them also to solicit work from other students in the fourth through eighth grades. Yet to the teacher's surprise, the new editors chose to include all of the younger students, even kindergartners. They did so eagerly, even though they knew it meant that they'd be taking on a lot more work, not only in the sheer number of submissions but in the extra time they'd have to spend to help the younger children polish their drafts. "We had all been 'buddy mentors,'" Rueter explained, referring to the school's requirement that seventh- and eighth-graders spend time hanging out with kindergartners. "So people were thinking of their buddies. When I was in seventh grade, I had a buddy I just loved. He inspired me to be a camp counselor; he opened that door for me, that I liked looking after kids. So of course I wanted to see what my buddy had to say."*

Forty-five students submitted drafts, which meant the editors needed to spend several extra hours in the late afternoons and evenings as they worked with hopeful young writers. To the teachers, it was clear that the older kids knew they were making a difference, not only in the lives of the students whose writing they selected, but in the spirit that prevailed at the school.

"The faculty had been a little apprehensive about the selection process," recalled the head of school, Peter Sommer. "But the kids were amazing. They went back to every student who had submitted something to give feedback about what they had written. It was a lot more than real literary journals do."

WE ARE FAMILY

The Cambridge students' generous decision didn't happen serendipitously. In several ways, both subtle and obvious, the private K–8 school makes a point of encouraging students to think of themselves as part of a caring community. This reflects both the spirit of the Quakers who founded the school in 1961 and of progressive reformers who reimagined American education some sixty years earlier, and whose philosophy the Cambridge Friends School today explicitly shares. "I'm proud to say we're progressive," says Sommer. "And to me this means a lot more than just the idea of dealing with the whole child, which we do. It means contributing to create a better society."

It bears repeating that this isn't merely a kind and compassionate way but quite a smart way to run a school. Evidence attests that far from being loosey-goosey, the work of building strong school communities makes hardheaded sense. I'm sure that one day some enterprising economist will be able to figure out the precise dollar value of inputs, in amount of time attending to school ties, versus outputs, in terms of avoided costs of high school dropouts, unemployment, and mental health expenses.

Remember that research I've mentioned that showed that students who feel emotionally connected to their schoolmates and teachers do better academically, in addition to avoiding substance abuse, depression, and early pregnancies? That longitudinal federal study is merely one example of abundant evidence of the value of strong school communities for elementary and middle school students, not only in improving student morale but in enhancing academic performance. As parents and teachers know only too well, children at this stage tend to be more easily influenced by peers than adults. A strong school community thus becomes a kind of crucible for forming character. Investments by teachers and principals in creating such communities pay off for schools all year long, while for students, the benefits may last a lifetime.

What makes this task all the more pressing are the discipline and morale problems plaguing American schools in recent decades. The rise in reported bullying and other misbehavior has led many schools to launch "zero tolerance" campaigns. Students have been suspended even for such minor offenses as cursing or shoving, which previously would at most have led to after-school detention or a meeting with parents.

The number of high school students suspended or expelled increased by roughly 40 percent between 1972–73 and 2009–10, according to researchers at the University of California at Los Angeles. Overall, however, these measures have failed to make classrooms more manageable, even as they've increased the number of children ending up in the justice system, and by far disproportionately punished African-American students over white students.

Beyond merely avoiding bad outcomes, community building at school nurtures personal qualities often touted as key twenty-first-century skills, such as communication, collaboration, and leadership. As usual, our twentieth-century progressive forebears understood this well. When the *Harvard Business Review* recently published a long article extolling the art of collaboration, with an air that this was all new material, I had to smile: the story may as well have been written by the progressive school founder Caroline Pratt.

Colonel Francis W. Parker and John Dewey both used the emotionally evocative phrase "embryonic community" to describe their ideal of a connected school. To me, this conveys two aspirations simultaneously: that schools can care for children much as a parent would; and that schools can build models of altruistic societies that may one day be replicated on larger scales. (Progressive educators are nothing if not optimistic.)

At the Winnetka schools in Illinois, superintendent Carleton Washburne strategically designed class projects that required "co-operative thinking and working." Washburne often referred to his goal of creating "social-mindedness" in children, so that they might learn "to identify their good with the good of the whole . . . an essential dimension of character."

A TOOLBOX FOR COMMUNITY BUILDERS

On my travels to progressive schools throughout America, I was inspired to see educators carrying on the tradition of building close-knit communities in which children learn to be both collaborators and leaders. It struck me again and again that so much of this work emerged directly from the shared, early foundation (literally!) of the classroom rug—that trusting, comfortable space where students can air their feelings, resolve conflicts, and envision themselves as part of a family, working toward mutually supportive goals.

Back home at Park Day School, our third-grade teacher, Mona Halaby, has written a book on this topic, *Belonging: Creating Community in the Classroom*. It tells of how she encourages her students to write notes in a confidential class book whenever they are worried about some conflict arising between classmates. At the end of each week, they gather on the rug—a tacit signal that they can relax and let their guard down—while Halaby reads through entries from the previous week, asking the class to work through the problems together, one at a time. It takes only a few weeks as a rule, she says, for the children to become skilled at collectively resolving their conflicts.

At the Children's Community School in Van Nuys, a similar strategy goes by the name of the "magic circle." As Neal Wrightson, the head of school, explained:

"When two kids have a conflict, we don't immediately assume that it's just the two of them who have to solve it. . . . Very often this is something that gets brought to the whole group, not that the whole group stands in judgment so much, but that the other students can support these two in figuring it out. It's that idea that you are in this community, and so you have some responsibility for any problems that are arising, even if you aren't directly connected to that specific incident or issue. Again, I think that's very much a part of being in a democracy."

Wrightson contrasted the problem-solving training his students receive with the current impasse in Washington, where, he says, "People say, 'It's just my way or the highway.' Being able to say, 'This is what I believe, but I'm willing to do this here because we have to accomplish this task and get this done,' only comes with practice."

That practice is encouraged in many different ways. At Park Day School and several of the other progressive schools on my tour, students are formally evaluated at the end of each term on their social and emotional development and ability to work well with others, just as they are on their academic progress and achievement.

At the Hubbard Woods Elementary School, part of the Winnetka School District, small groups of first- through fourth-graders and two adult staff members remain together as a "family" throughout those early years, the better to work on relationship building and conflict resolution.

Reliable rituals help bind communities together. And here I'd urge heads of schools to think beyond the classic school assembly hour or Spirit Day, even though some may not want to follow the lengths to which I've gone. At Park Day School, every year on the day before Thanksgiving break children have been expected to clean their classrooms thoroughly to prepare for a Special Visitors Day. Afterwards, I have made an appearance, elaborately dressed up as a magician, or giant rabbit, or even, one year, as a nun, to conduct my "white glove inspection." Tut-tutting in a falsetto voice, I've run my fingers along window sills and desks until my gloves turned gray, yet always congratulated the children on their efforts. The kids routinely have had so much fun that they have forgotten to complain about all the work.

Progressive schools aren't shy about reminding students of the ways they are connected. At Mission Hill in Boston, one teacher posts pictures of individual students alongside lists of their hopes and dreams, and then ties green string between the children whose lists match. Together with many other progressive schools, Mission Hill also puts up motivational posters to remind children of common goals. One of these is a list called "The Five Habits of Mind," compiled by founder Deborah Meier, enumerating the key intellectual skills that each student should work to develop. The five keywords on this list point to questions that students should be asking themselves as they learn something new. They are: Significance (Why is this important?), Perspective (What is the point of view?), Evidence (How do you know this is true?), Connection (How is this relevant?), and Supposition (What if this were different?). The Five Habits of Mind posters remind students that they are working as a group to become more skillful and intentional learners.

More broadly, progressive teachers are constantly asking students to imagine a better world for themselves. At Park Day, at the start of each school year, our teachers ask their students to describe the kind of classroom they want, and then turn their answers into informal contracts, known as class agreements. One of my favorites, written by a group of fifth-graders, reads: "In order to have a respectful, accepting, fact-filled, awesome classroom where we all feel safe and flabbergasted, we agree to listen to each other and pay attention."

On Susan Erb's first-grade classroom walls, a boy named Bruno has written: "When someone gets hurt, I want everyone to help them." Another student, Marco, says, "I want this place to be friendly and nobody to fight. I want to have fun in here and I don't want anyone stepping on books or stepping on everything."

STEP BY STEP

The art of building strong communities at school requires adults to be sensitive to children's developing abilities. Progressive educators see child development as the gradual process of a human becoming less self-centered. For a kindergartner, this means understanding that his or her classmates have feelings of their own. By third grade, students are developing the ability to assess how their class is getting along as a group. By fifth grade, they may better understand their own roles in that dynamic.

From our students' first day at school, we nudge them along in this process. Teachers ask kindergartners to notice if anyone on the playground doesn't have a playmate, and imagine how that might feel. First-graders learn the slogan, "If you see something wrong, do something about it." These are tall orders for egocentric five- and six-year-olds, but our job is to challenge them to grow. We don't hand out stickers on charts for this kind of progress. Instead, we call on children's intrinsic empathy, nurturing a sense of reward from within.

Whenever we can, we enlist older students in this effort. That's why many progressive schools include classes that combine students who may be a year or two apart, or at least have buddy programs like the one that meant so much to Sam Rueter at the Cambridge Friends School. The idea may seem old-fashioned, reminiscent of one-room schoolhouses. Yet modern researchers have recognized its value, particularly for children who may learn at faster or slower paces than their age group, and feel more permission to move at their own speed in a mixed-age class. Studies have found that multi-age classes can increase children's self-confidence and enthusiasm about going to school. As with most progressive teaching methods, however, this tactic usually requires more work from teachers, in the form of more attention to each student.

The Wingra School in Madison, Wisconsin, is one of several progressive schools in which students routinely spend two years with the same teacher. Head of school Paul Brahce says he's seen the "elders"—those in their second year of the program— happily take on the task of orienting newcomers, while all the students benefit from a closer and more familiar relationship with their teacher.

Park Day School doesn't have multi-age classes, but we do have buddy programs, and I've often witnessed the powerful benefits that can come from putting older kids in positions of leadership. In short, it often brings out the best in them. A textbook case is that of our Sierra Leone–born student, Lansana Lapia.

Lapia was adopted at age eight by an American physician, Ian Zlotolow, and his girlfriend Wendy Cohen. Soldiers had killed his mother a few years earlier, after which Lapia was bitten on the leg by a venomous snake. At the time Zlotolow found him, abandoned in a hospital, Lapia was suffering from an infection that had led to osteomyelitis, a deterioration of bone tissue. Zlotolow brought the boy back to the United States, where he endured more than a dozen surgeries. His determination was such that he was playing basketball by the time he enrolled at Park Day.

Lapia attended our school during a particularly tumultuous time of his already eventful life. He was a Muslim immigrant—with the unusual name of Lansana Cohen Zlotolow Lapia—in a nation still shaken by the 9/11 attacks of five years earlier. His adoptive parents had separated, and he was shuttling back and forth between their homes while undergoing surgery after surgery.

At Park Day, however, Lapia was known for his radiant grin. I often saw him playing basketball and soccer with the younger children. It's common at Park Day, though rare at many other schools, for kids of different ages to play together. And for Lapia, it seemed like a healing experience. The last I heard of him, he was attending Berkeley High, where in his freshman year he was named the most inspirational player on the basketball team.

R-E-S-P-E-C-T

The annals of rock are full of adolescent anger at feeling powerless and disrespected at school. Consider Pink Floyd's "Another Brick in the Wall" and the Ramones' "I Don't Wanna Be

Learned/I Don't Wanna Be Tamed." The resentment has fueled not only musical creativity but all sorts of misbehavior, from truancy to graffiti to bullying.

In contrast, I've seen students happily "be learned" when they feel they have some control over their daily environment. The more respect and control we can give them—in accordance with their developmental capacity—the better. Skilled teachers know how to do this, while also maintaining relatively orderly classrooms. At Park Day and many other progressive schools, teachers call students by their first names—and vice versa. It's rare in a progressive school for students past the first grade to have to raise their hands to go to the bathroom, and it's also rare for the children to abuse that privilege. Nor will you hear school bells ringing at the end of each forty-minute block; students are expected to be responsible enough to know where and when they need to go.

Teachers at all the schools I visited convey their high expectations for students, beginning on the first day of school. At Mission Hill School, for instance, kindergarten teacher Kathy D'Andrea begins each day with a morning meeting, in which a student takes attendance. D'Andrea might then propose a joint project—say, the students could create a book about recycling out of recycled materials. She'll ask for a show of hands to demonstrate interest, and then will discuss whether there was a consensus or not. Students can pick the activities they want to work on for the next couple of hours, with some practicing parts in a play, others writing in their journals. Like most adults, they tend to participate with much more enthusiasm when they have some choice in the matter.

As students at progressive schools mature, they're allowed increasing autonomy. At The Children's School in Chicago, the K–5 students run their own daily assemblies, with adults only rarely intervening. On the morning I observed, a third-grade girl was conducting the meeting with all the confidence of an adult, formally welcoming me to the school and handling the daily announcements. As at other progressive schools, students are regularly assigned jobs normally reserved for adults, such as leading visitors on tours, and they do so with great competence and pride.

Many of the progressive high schools I visited included students as members of the board of trustees, albeit with limited voting rights—the idea being that you cultivate leadership in students by putting them into positions where they can both observe adults as leaders and practice those skills themselves. At the same time, many progressive schools avoid traditional forms of student government. Progressive faculties usually prefer not to isolate a small group of students as nominal leaders, a choice students tend to support. At Park Day, I was pleased to learn that our middle-schoolers had turned down their teachers' suggestion that they form a student government, saying they thought leadership should be required of all students and not delegated to a few.

It's worth recalling that Progressive Education was born at a time when the saying "Spare the rod and spoil the child" passed for wisdom, and children who misbehaved at home or in school were routinely beaten. Mark Twain, who grew up in Hannibal, Missouri , wrote tellingly of this practice and its counterproductive results in *The Adventures of Tom Sawyer* (1876), which was reissued during the Progressive Era's heyday:

> *Mr. Dobbin's lashings were very vigorous ones. He seemed to take a vindictive pleasure in punishing the least shortcomings. The consequence was, that the smaller boys spent their days in terror and suf-*

ferings and their nights in plotting revenge. They threw away no
opportunity to do the master a mischief.

As head of school at Park Day, I did my best to understand
and work with children who were repeatedly misbehaving, a
strategy I'm convinced is more effective—and today, of course,
more law-abiding—than lashings. It's been said that kids who
get labeled as troublemakers are looking for attention. The
trick, I believe, is to *give* them attention, but not in a way that
either rewards them or shames them for their misbehavior.
When students were repeatedly disruptive in class, they would
have to visit my office once or twice a day, where I offered them
a glass jar and a choice of red blocks or green. The child would
have to choose a block to place in the jar. Green meant that the
morning had been peaceful; red, that there'd been a problem
that we needed to discuss. It was a very simple way of encouraging self-monitoring and self-control, and usually, after a few
days, the child would be able to take pride in seeing the green
blocks accumulate inside the jar.

I've yet to meet a progressive educator who believes in managing children by fear, much less by corporal punishment, even in
cases of severe misbehavior. Ayla Gavins, at Mission Hill, says that
by far the majority of discipline issues at her school are handled
by talking to the children responsible for the transgressions. In
her eight years as head of school, Gavins has never expelled a student, although she has suspended children in rare cases for what
she calls acts of "unwarranted, premeditated cruelty." Such
instances, she says, always involve extensive conversations with the
student and his or her parents, and a strict re-entry plan.

"I don't like having kids out of school, for all kinds of reasons," Gavins said. "They belong at school. I don't want them on
the streets." So Gavins tries more creative strategies, such as

pairing an older child with a teacher who works with younger children, making the offending child, under close supervision, responsible for helping to care for the younger kids.

As Gavins reminds us, children's misbehavior is rarely as simple as it may seem at first. She told of a recent incident in which a sixth-grade girl had picked up a pair of scissors and was going to cut off another girl's hair. "From the outside, it looks like there's this dangerous girl in the room, and we have to get her out. But as we know, the story matters. And it turns out the other girls had been pushing her to her limit, which they had found out was pretty easy to do." The incident led to conferences with all of the students involved, and their parents, while Gavins took the opportunity to remind teachers of their need to pay special attention to explosive children, to watch for signs of an impending meltdown and to coach the students to "use their words" instead of fists or scissors.

When it comes to coping with bullying, I've been dismayed by the clumsiness of some of the top-down directives to schools in recent years. Some states, for instance, have passed laws that oblige school staffs to immediately report if they see anything that even remotely looks like bullying, preventing teachers from using their best judgment about the kinds of incidents that merit intervention. While of course students need to be protected from mistreatment, "bullying" has become a buzzword, making parents, teachers, and students feel defensive and, sometimes, overreactive. From my perspective, you can have all the top-down legislation in the world, and it will only be a Band-Aid unless you've done the work to build a culture where bullying won't thrive. When students aren't feeling ignored or bored by stifling routines, and instead are given respect and some degree of autonomy, and are truly engaged with their learning, bullying and other misbehavior become much less problematic.

I'm not saying we haven't had some problems with bullying at Park Day. Back in 2004, when national concern over the issue was growing, we made a special effort to raise awareness and make sure it didn't become a major problem. We held meetings with students and parents to discuss what bullying is and how best to prevent it and cope with it. Our second-graders joined with peers from the Emerson School, the public school two blocks away from us, to design and write a pamphlet titled *Stop Bullying in Elementary School*, which we shared with other local schools. Children also produced anti-bullying skits that they performed in neighboring classrooms.

In recent years, all of our teachers have held weekly class meetings during which kids are encouraged to talk about any incidents in which students have been teased or bullied. The kids responsible for the misbehavior can then apologize and make amends. This approach is known as "restorative justice," and it's becoming more popular even at conventional schools, as evidence has mounted that suspending and expelling students ultimately causes more harm than good. California schools have led the way in this trend, with encouraging results: during the 2012–13 school year, on average, state schools reported a 14 percent drop in suspensions.

BEYOND TOLERANCE

You can't build strong communities in which students disparage each other for their differences, such as those pertaining to sex or race. That's just one reason why progressive educators by and large are hypervigilant about any signs of such intolerance.

Diversity is in our DNA, given that many of the early progressive schools were founded by first-wave feminists, who encouraged their female students to excel at a time when even sending girls to public school was still a little daring.

Today, of course, girls by many measures are outperforming boys in school, and have fewer problems being treated as equals. But progressive schools are once again on the cutting edge of social change—in this case, in working to build a safe and accepting environment for gay, lesbian, and transgender students.

Park Day School has been part of this civil rights frontier since 2002, when we enrolled our first transgender kindergartner. Born female, he began to identify as male in preschool, at which time his parents told us they wanted to enroll him as a boy. The family had sought us out because of our reputation as a school that embraces diversity. We already had enrolled several students with two parents of the same sex, while our teaching practices included encouraging children to write essays on famous gay people such as Michelangelo, and to write Dear Abby–style letters to imaginary gay children who had been teased on the playground.

Nonetheless, when I first saw this application come across my desk, I knew we had a lot of learning to do.

A major change in attitudes was only just dawning in this nation, where traditionally children identifying themselves as different from their gender at birth have been punished by their parents, or, at best, sent to counseling, to "straighten them out." At Park Day, we were paying attention to national experts quoted in the media as expressing alarm at the high rate of depression among such children—by some estimates, one in four will attempt suicide—and warning families to accept kids for who they say they are. Then we had to figure out what that meant for Park Day. We've since been told that we were the first school in the nation to address this problem openly, and our efforts earned a mention on the front page of the *New York Times*.

It was our good fortune at the time that Stephanie Brill, who would go on to become the nation's leading expert on transgender children, was also a parent at our school. Back then, Brill was running a hospital-based support group for families, some of whom were coping with the aftermath of a suicide attempt by a child as young as six or seven years old. Over the next few years, she would become founder and director of Gender Spectrum, which offers advice to parents and schools, and write the first guidebook on raising children who identify with the opposite gender of their birth, or in some cases, with both genders or none at all.

Brill is used to skeptics pointing out that some preschoolers go through phases where they may imagine they are other than they are, even pretending to be a cat or a dog, but she says, "This is different. We're talking about an identity that is consistent and persistent—such that the child doesn't forget even when waking from a nightmare."

Such children can present daunting challenges at school. It's there where conflicts with peers most often first turn up, and if handled poorly by adults can wreak long-term emotional damage. Should teachers encourage children to "come out" about their differences, or to hide them or play them down? Which bathroom should they use? What cabin should they stay in on overnight trips? How much should teachers talk about the issue in sex education classes? What's the best way to counsel anxious parents?

We held several training sessions with Brill and other specialists for our teachers, in addition to workshops for students and parents. Brill alerted us to nuances we never would have thought of on our own, persuading our teachers to learn gender-neutral vocabulary and to line up students according to the color of their shoes rather than by gender. One of my own sensitivity challenges came early on, when Brill politely suggested I needed to end what had been a longtime school tradition of my "Aim Straight Club," part of an effort for boys to keep school bathrooms clean.

Today, most of the bathrooms at Park Day School are considered gender-neutral. The bathrooms for the lower grades don't say "Boys" or "Girls" but have images of a sun and a moon—and the kids can use whichever room they want. There are also some added single stalls for privacy. Our school was obviously ahead of the rest of the nation on this issue, but some parts of the country are catching up. In January 2014, California became the first American state to detail the rights of transgender students by statute, including letting them choose which bathroom to use. The education departments of Connecticut and Massachusetts have implemented similar policies by fiat.

Our reputation for taking this issue seriously made us immediately attractive to other parents of transgender children, and one of our initial quandaries was whether to accept every such child, and dramatically skew our student population. We chose initially to go slowly, but eventually decided it was most important that such children have a welcoming, safe place to go to school: today Park Day enrolls approximately half a dozen transgender students. Rather than stepping back, we've stepped up our efforts to encourage understanding and welcoming of such children. Meanwhile, I've gotten calls, seeking advice, from heads of school all over the country.

I think of Park Day's attitude toward diversity as going "beyond tolerance." That's because I envision a community that isn't merely accepting of differences, as if some of its members are inherently worthier than others, and acting from a sense of *noblesse oblige*. Rather, my goal is a school that respects and even celebrates differences. Toward that end, one of our earliest gestures as a school committed to welcoming transgender students was to dedicate a week in 2002 to a series of upbeat activities geared to understanding and appreciating gender differences.

Our young students were treated to songs about pride and a rendition of *Sesame Street*'s "Rubber Ducky" performed by the Gay Men's Chorus, which in its twenty-four-year history had never before been invited to perform at a school. In classrooms decorated with rainbow flags, we hosted more than forty different speakers from the Bay Area's gay leadership, including KFOG disc jockey Dave Morey and the East Bay high-end chocolate maker John Scharffenberger. A lesbian veterinarian and a lesbian Baptist minister spoke, as did a transgender therapist. Former San Francisco supervisor Harry Britt spoke about growing up lonely and closeted in Texas. We chose our speakers strategically, with the idea that when, at some future time, our students encountered homophobia, they'd remember all the wonderful people they'd met—skilled singers and people who worked with chocolate and animals—and reflect on how such hatred would hurt them. We got ribbed a little in the subsequent article published in the *San Francisco Chronicle*, which said that Park Day elementary students may be unique in the nation for having spelling lists that include the words "lesbian," "homosexual," and "transgender." But not one parent complained, and a few called to thank us.

"It was a pretty wild idea," recalled Michael Pollan, whose son Isaac enrolled in fifth grade several months later. "People came to the campus and talked about sex changes and taking hormones." The extraordinary attention to gender differences at Park Day "blew Isaac's mind," Pollan added, "but in a good way, on balance. He had grown up until then in a lily-white, homogenous community, and this was part of his socialization. Today, he's comfortable with all kinds of differences."

America's progressive schools are justifiably proud of the efforts we have made to include students of all races, ethnic groups, income levels, and gender identities. Honestly, sometimes the harder challenge is to guarantee a mix of political opinions. Our heads of schools and teachers tend to wear our hearts on our sleeves, and as you've probably gleaned by now, they aren't as a rule hearts inclined to classically conservative values. Still, one of *our* foremost values is that everyone involved in our schools should have a voice. As Peter Sommer, at Cambridge Friends, notes: "I knew we were succeeding two years ago, when a graduate told me he was able to be a Republican here."

DEMOCRACY ISN'T JUST FOR STUDENTS

History buffs may find it ironic that a movement that puts such a premium on democratic governance for students has been led, at least in some schools, by autocratic principals who often fiercely resisted sharing power with other adults, be they teachers or parents. "I have been accused to my face of hating parents, of wishing all children could be born orphans," acknowledged Caroline Pratt. In her early years running the City and Country School in New York, Pratt admitted that she indeed would often walk around the block so as not to run into a parent she feared would want to pester her about whether she was effectively preparing her students for high school. Even so, she went on to say she couldn't imagine a more "co-conspiratorial, hand-in-glove" relationship than the students' parents maintained with their teachers.

By their nature, progressive schools attract teachers as well as heads of school with strong personalities. At the same time, I think it's fair to say that progressive educators' fervent belief in the value of democratic collaboration often compels us to muster the patience to consider others' viewpoints—be they colleagues or parents—no matter how much work that sometimes takes.

"You need to be comfortable with the slow pace of change," Joseph Marshall, head of the Orchard School in Indianapolis, told me on my visit to his independent pre-K–8 campus. "It takes time and humility to recognize that you need to be in constant conversation with others as you approach decisions."

This can often be one of the trickiest parts of the job for school heads. Obviously, not all decisions can be made by committee, and it takes wisdom to know which ones those are and diplomacy to explain decisions in their wake. The one indispensable tool in this endeavor is open, clear, and frequent communication between heads of schools and teachers, heads of schools and parents, teachers and parents, and students. As Ayla Gavins has said, "Everything I do is visible. So there are no secrets. There is no hiding, and no backroom deals. Everyone knows what my work is, and because that's the expectation of everyone here—that everyone's work is public—everyone is expected to defend their work. And that's also true for me."

No one ever said democracy is easy. But through the years, what's often been harder for many of our students has been to reconcile themselves to the less idealistic world outside of our embryonic societies. As the *Harvard Crimson* observed back in 1958, in an article about the Putney School, a graduate of that institution often finds it difficult "to cope with what he considers the mediocrity of life. It is the necessary price to be paid for having been shown the possibilities of one 'better world.' "

Such frustration isn't our goal, of course. Rather, as I'll elaborate later in this book, we hope that those who have experienced our idealistic communities will emerge with the skills and the determination to recreate caring and collaborative democracies wherever they next study, work, and live.

CHAPTER 5

The Storyboard
The Progressive Heart of High Technology

Third-grader Sophie Orston and the storyboard for "Sophie's
Fight Game," at the Galloway School in Atlanta.
Photograph by Mark Gerl

We must play the game of learning—not the game of school.

—School founder ELLIOTT GALLOWAY (1920–2008)

SOPHIE'S FIGHT GAME

Sophie Orston was all of eight years old when she designed her first video game. Against a mauve sky, a brown vampire bat with two prominent white teeth moves back and forth over a scampering orange cat, to an electronically generated hip-hop beat. Every so often, the bat drops a ball. The task for the player is to move the cat so as not to get hit. When the cat does get hit, it makes an "ow!" noise, which Sophie recorded herself.

Designing the game, with a program developed by the Massachusetts Institute of Technology, called on several different skills, including writing and designing the "storyboard" where Sophie planned her script, just as a professional game designer would do, and some math, art, and music. "Every week, there was something new," as Sophie recalls. "I had to figure out who the good guy was, and then who'd be the bad guy, and then I had to pick the music. . . ."

On days when kids weren't working online, Sophie's teacher, Mark Gerl, a self-described "old-school geek" in a NASA T-shirt, arranged Skype interviews for his class with panels of computer engineers. Meanwhile, to encourage the girls in his class, Gerl also slipped in commentary on some of history's lesser-known computer science heroines, including Ada Lovelace, often described as the world's first computer programmer; Grace Hopper, a pioneer computer scientist and U.S. Navy rear admiral; and Hedy Lamarr, an Austrian actress and inventor whose work paved the way for modern wireless communications. (Lamarr's 1941 invention—in tandem with the composer George Antheil, of an early technique for frequency hopping, was considered vital to America's defense in World War II.)

Gerl, the son, grandson, and great-grandson of teachers, has worked at the Galloway School for the past twelve years. He is an unabashed fan of Progressive Education, having first heard about John Dewey from his grandmother and mother. As an undergraduate, he became fascinated with the somewhat obscure sixteenth century Moravian educa-

tional reformer John Amos Comenius, who is credited with introducing the first pictorial textbooks written in languages other than Latin, and who opposed the practice of rote memorization in schools. Gerl believes the difference between conventional and progressive schools' modern attitudes toward technology is that conventional schools tend to teach students to use PowerPoint so they'll know how to use PowerPoint, while progressive schools teach students to use PowerPoint so they'll be able to express ideas that fascinate them.

Sophie is new to the Galloway School, having transferred from a more conventional school that didn't teach programming and where, she notes, the teachers were generally less inspiring. Often, these days, she says, she lies on her bed at home and thinks about the kind of life she'll lead as an adult. She's interested in singing, art, and inventing things. Asked if there is any job that girls can't do, she touches her cheek in surprise at the question. "No," she says. "I can't think of any." She's just as surprised by the suggestion that some kids her age don't like school. "I love it," she says. "I'm having tons of fun."

WE'RE NO LUDDITES

Progressive educators are often stereotyped as being automatically opposed to technology, like the nineteenth-century English Luddites who smashed textile machines to try to stall the Industrial Revolution from throwing artisans out of jobs. The image may have fit us, or some of us, in the past, but it was never entirely accurate. Many decades ago, John Dewey himself noted progressive educators' duty to prepare students "not for the world of the past, not for our world, but for their world—the world of the future."

Today, there are many good reasons to keep that admonition in mind. Computers and other forms of high technology are now ubiquitous and all but indispensable in the workplace and in our social lives. To ignore them would shortchange our students, failing to prepare them for their futures. Technology fascinates our students. Whether we like it or not, it's a leading way they have fun outside of school. So if we want them to have fun *inside* school, as we most certainly do, to hook them on learning, we'd simply better find ways to deal with whatever personal reservations we have about the growing number of hours that all of us these days are spending plugged in to various devices. Let me be clear: we do have some strong reservations. Many of us, myself included, cringe when we see a child sitting in front of a computer, in charge of the mouse, with others gathered around, simply watching. We also worry about the ways computer technology provides instant, even addicting, rewards. I could go on . . . but like everything that takes place in the classroom, taking advantage of technology requires vigilance, good judgment, and a constant balancing of risks and rewards. And I do see irresistible rewards to be gained from children's natural excitement about these novel tools.

As the Galloway School puts it in its guiding philosophy, children learn best when they are drawn rather than pushed into learning. Thus, if what initially draws Sophie Orston into learning about computer science is the thrill of a "punch and fight" video game, we can work with that. It's an easy introduction into learning how computers work.

I'm no techie myself, which may be an understatement. I got my first desktop computer in the late 1980s, and taught myself how to use it with a tutorial on floppy disks, but since then I've been content to call IT support whenever I have problems. I'm a digital immigrant, not a native, content to let my twenty-something son, Matt, be the family expert.

Still, I can fully appreciate the ways in which all kinds of high-tech advances in schools not only fit with Progressive Education philosophy but provide exciting new opportunities for our schools. To the extent that they keep students as the "center of gravity," which indeed they uniquely can do, computers are the ultimate progressive tool. That's why, on my tour of progressive schools throughout the country, I was so happy to see so many of us on the cutting edge of integrating high technology in our classrooms in thoughtful, farsighted ways.

At the Wickliffe Elementary School, for instance, which is not only one of America's rare progressive public schools but the only school I know of that features the word "progressive" right on the sign on its building, students have learned to use digital photography tools to advocate for their interests. A video produced by third-graders, called *The Pencil Story*, details the students' concerns about substandard pencils that resisted being sharpened and had lead that broke too easily and erasers that kept popping off. The students' video persuaded the manufacturer to change its production processes and ship a new supply of pencils to the school.

At the Bank Street School for Children, an independent, pre-K through eighth-grade school in New York City, students communicate by Skype with computer pals in China, trading photographs and notes about how they spent their weekend and what they had for lunch. At the Cambridge School of Weston, a boarding and day high school, students report to a Youth Understanding Media (YUM) Lab for classes in digital photography, film-scoring, and computerized design. The entire campus is wired, and teachers use interactive whiteboards for their lessons, while also encouraging students to blog online and debate each other on schoolwide Web forums. Across town in Cambridge, Shady Hill School science teacher Barbara Bratzel has incorporated a sophisticated design program called LabView to assist middle school students in creating graphic representations for the science concepts they're studying. Even the bucolic Putney School in Vermont boasts a new Instructional Technology Center, where students use video production equipment, music composition applications, video-conferencing, and desktop publishing tools to create professional-quality reports for their classes. They also can study robotics and geographic information systems, and tap innovative data collection techniques for their science classes.

Remember, our pioneers were fervent fans of science, optimistic about the role of new discoveries in creating a better world. They were also among the earliest champions of vocational education—and nowadays we can't be blind to the fact that computers are central to most jobs.

Having computers in schools also fits with Dewey's notion that school should be more like life. Again, whether adults approve or not, most kids today are plugged into some kind of device during much of their free time. Their teachers can and should help them figure out how to manage and get the best out of these new advances. At the same time, computers and other high-tech communications technologies serve our progressive agenda in that they're powerful tools for building communities, enabling online conversations among classmates and teachers. They can also make it easier for students to learn at their own pace and by various means—not just through text, but via pictures, videos, and spoken words. They make it easier and faster for students to reflect on and revise their work, and allow them to reach out beyond classroom walls, even all the way to China, as the Bank Street students have done.

Still, what may be most progressive of all about computers is the way they encourage student autonomy, changing the role of the teacher from the sage on-the-stage to a coach. Fostering independence among students is a central goal of Progressive Education. At the Galloway School, Gerl says he never gives his class detailed instructions. "I say, you're going to make your video game and you're going to tell me when it's done," he says. "The only time I limit them is when they want to do fifty levels with eight hundred enemies. Then I tell them, you've got three months, so maybe you can do two levels and one enemy." A poster in the computer lab tells students who have questions to ask two friends before they ask their teacher. Says Gerl: "I want them to figure things out on their own as much as possible. I have them looking up examples in reference books and asking each other for help and advice. I'm really the last resort."

In a study based on tests of more than 13,000 students, Educational Testing Services researcher Harold Wenglinsky demonstrated that the effectiveness of computers in the classroom depended on the way in which they were used. If relied on for conventional goals, such as to aid in drilling for tests, computers in the classroom actually tended to reduce student achievement. Yet if used in more creative ways, such as to help students simulate conditions with changing variables, they improved it.

At their best, as research has confirmed, new communications technologies make learning more enticing, dynamic, empowering, and effective. Studies have found that under certain circumstances, students involved in multimedia projects outperform students who don't use technology when it comes to communication skills, teamwork, and problem solving. I'm particularly impressed by some of the recent findings from the Khan Academy, the Silicon Valley–based creator of online tutorials, which lets students watch instructional videos at home so that they can dedicate class time to working on problems, together with teachers and fellow classmates. After one of our near neighbors, the public charter Oakland Unity High School, began using the tutorials on a pilot basis in 2011, students doubled their class average score on an algebra test, while math teachers reported that kids were becoming more confident, putting more effort into their work, and taking more responsibility for their own learning.

THE EDTECH BANDWAGON

For the past several years, throughout America, conventional and unconventional schools alike have been scrambling to figure out the best ways to incorporate new technologies and keep up with an accelerating rate of change. One of the few things that's clear is that more technology in the classroom is inevitable.

In June 2013, President Obama announced his goal of providing high-speed wireless connections to 99 percent of U.S. classrooms within five years. Last I looked, major U.S. high-tech firms, including Apple, Microsoft, Sprint, and Verizon, had donated more than $750 million to the cause.

Already by 2012, more than 2.5 million public school students were taking at least one online course, compared to just 750,000 five years earlier. Sixty-five percent of schools reported that they had a "digital-content strategy." More strong evidence of the changes underway is that when the first nationwide student tests based on the new Core State Standards were given in 2014, they were computerized rather than printed on paper multiple-choice forms. The test-takers were all expected to know how to use computer word-processing programs.

Now, to some extent, we've been through this movie before. During the dot.com boom of the late 1990s, computer companies poured money into schools, conveying great expectations that desktops and word processing would transform learning.

The bottom line: they didn't. So forgive me if my enthusiasm is tempered with caution and even some skepticism. I worry when I see schools—including some progressive schools—jumping on the bandwagon of purchasing iPads en masse without a lot of thoughtful planning as to how they might be used. The trick is always to make sure that any new devices will encourage rather than thwart students' sense of engagement and empowerment, so that we don't justify Henry David Thoreau's stark assessment, in the mid-nineteenth century, that "Men have become the tools of their tools." Or to be more specific: the tools of the toolmakers.

While most progressive educators I know aren't excessively suspicious of computers per se, as a rule we're plenty wary of computer and software and network manufacturers, many of whom are as ruthlessly profit-minded as the robber barons of the early twentieth century. It makes me nervous to hear financial titans smacking their lips over the profits to be made from public education, as News Corp. executive Rupert Murdoch was heard to do in 2011, when he estimated the K–12 education market as worth $500 billion a year. Two years later, Murdoch's company, Amplify, unveiled its new computerized tablet, intended for millions of American schoolchildren and their teachers. Amplify vendors touted the potential benefits of the new device in reducing the hours teachers spend on administrative chores, while some teachers worried that reducing their hours would also reduce their numbers.

They have good reason for concern. Some critics worry that the new technology provides new ways to spy on teachers, monitoring their use of time down to the minute. And in some cases, computers have indeed replaced teachers altogether. Take the case of Rocketship, a San Jose, California, based chain of charter schools that has won national praise for raising the test scores of its mostly low-income pupils, with a blend of traditional teaching and online instruction. The charter has made ends meet by assigning fewer teachers per pupil—reportedly up to one hundred children in a class in the online labs. Progressive educators always prioritize the student-teacher relationship over time spent at the keyboard. Yet today's sometimes unconstrained enthusiasm for technology has led even Microsoft's Bill Gates to insist that "Technology is just a tool. In terms of getting the kids working together and motivating them, the teacher is the most important."

At Park Day School, we have a technology innovation committee that is constantly assessing new devices, from computer tablets to laser cutters and 3-D printers, through a progressive lens. Keeping the child at the center of our vision, we ask whether more time spent with gizmos is developmentally appropriate—young children, in particular, need time to explore the world with their hands—and whether there are other, more important things that students should be doing with their time. Keeping in mind our commitment to social justice, we also evaluate potential purchases with an eye toward their environmental impact, and whether they are manufactured in ways that respect workers' welfare. More and more, we need to also ask ourselves whether our decisions will serve to nurture children's creativity or merely encourage a culture of acquisitiveness.

CRAFTINESS

The word "technology" comes from the Greek τέχνη, translated as "craft," "craftsmanship," or "art." Many progressive educators would say this is our primary interest when it comes to all forms of technology, high and low, and, indeed, it is a crucial distinction.

You can see what I mean every autumn at Park Day School, when our parents and staff host a "Mini-Maker Faire," an off-shoot of the larger annual Maker Faire born in San Mateo, California, in 2006, and currently held in some one hundred cities around the world, with a Faire at the White House in the works. We held our first event in October 2011, and it immediately became my favorite time of the year: a celebration of hands-on skill, from apple cider–making to metal-smithing to robotics design, with rapt children rushing from booth to magic booth, firing model rockets, making jewelry, churning butter, and silk-screening T-shirts to the strains of our middle-schoolers' guitar band and the smell of greasy BBQ sausage. (I'm sure there have been healthier odors, too, but they're harder to detect. This is no vegans-only event.)

I credit the Faire's origins to two of our school's main assets: our sprawling campus in the heart of Oakland, and our exceptionally bright and engaged parents. There were two main mothers of invention for this project: Sabrina Merlo, a marketing director who later became program director for the Maker Faire in San Francisco and New York; and Jennifer Pahlka, then the founder of the national non-profit Code for America, which helps city governments adapt to the Internet age. At this writing, Pahlka is serving in the White House, as deputy chief technology officer for government innovation.

I remember when Merlo first approached me with the idea, contending that a hands-on festival would be more appealing and suited to our young families than our annual Garden Tour, which had been our main fund-raiser for the previous twenty years. I was thumbs-up from the beginning; as Merlo recalls today, I never even asked her for a budget.

From our first event, it was obvious that I was right to trust in Merlo and Pahlka's plan. Despite a deluge of rain that lasted through most of the Faire, nearly 3,000 people turned out—with kids stomping around in their rain boots—making it a huge success. I wore a leather rain hat, rain jacket, and boots, but was thoroughly soaked by nine thirty in the morning. It made me feel like a nine-year-old frolicking in the stormy weather that never let up all day. And frolic I did: if that many people were willing to show up during a torrential storm, we could only imagine the crowds that might come on a clear day.

Even though we sold Faire tickets at a fraction of the price of the Garden Tour, we got ten times the turnout, reaping three times the revenues from the tickets and a percentage of the concessions. What's more, our fund-raising is now much more aligned with our progressive principles, supporting artistry, invention, and a stand against a culture of commodification. "When all of life is for sale, it is a revolutionary act to become a maker of things," writes Wendy Tremayne, a Maker Faire champion and author of *The Good Life Lab: Radical Experiments in Hands-On Living.* As she elaborates: "Makers are in a position to understand and change the world. Buyers of things need only know where to find what they want and have the money to pay for what they're buying: acculturated knowledge. But makers of things know what things are made of, how they work, where they come from, what their real cost is, how to fix them. . . ."

Ilya Pratt, our learning specialist at Park Day School, has helped lead the local Maker movement, serving as a member of our technology innovation committee. In her spare time, Pratt rides and repairs bicycles. In a typically farsighted comment, she portrays the Maker movement as something more than a revolt against the power of corporations: it is also a creative response to the needs of the future, given concerns about a recent deficit of inventors and engineers—people who know how to work with their hands and come up with new things through exploration.

Of course, it's something else too: a healthy investment in children's brains. Once again, researchers have turned up intriguing evidence that this progressive affinity toward working with your hands not only can help make you sharper but less vulnerable to depression. After all, we humans have spent most of our history using our hands to make things: the Information Age that has us crouching over keyboards is an evolutionarily recent anomaly.

Ilya Pratt was so inspired by the new Maker energy at Park Day that she drew up a proposal to submit to still other remarkable parents at our school, who have a family philanthropy called the Abundance Foundation. Her original idea was to find support for teacher training so as to encourage design thinking among Park Day students. Out of this came connections with researchers at the Harvard Graduate School of Education, and pretty soon we had a new partnership.

Since 2012, Harvard has sent investigators to Park Day four times a year to study the origins of creativity and critical thinking in our students, while we have sent teachers to Harvard to keep them on the cutting edge of developing these qualities. The researchers come from a program called Project Zero, co-founded in 1967 by the celebrated Harvard psychologist Howard Gardner, who has done pioneering work on multiple intelligences. (The name refers to the fact that so little was known at that time about the origins of creativity.) Shari Tishman, the project's director, has said that Park Day School's long history of rich, hands-on learning activities made us a great match for this work, which has since expanded to include four other local schools, with Park Day the only private school among the five. "There's a tremendous encouragement of risk-taking and imagination and commitment to letting students pursue their curiosity and develop their own interests, becoming independent thinkers," Tishman says.

As part of the partnership, the Harvard project has piloted a program called DesignME, which stands for "design, make, engage," at Park Day and the Oakland International High School, a nearby public school. DesignME encourages students to design solutions to real-world problems. In one "design challenge," for instance, students used math and technology skills and very basic materials such as tape and drinking straws to get a model of a bird across the room on a wire, in order to study the science of movement. The project not only offers students confidence-building engineering challenges, but helps researchers understand how design thinking emerges in elementary school and middle school children. Previously such studies had only been done with high school students.

SHOP CULTURE

Looking back at our history, it's easy to see how progressive schools' modern embrace of technology, design, and invention is a natural outgrowth of shop class, which the forefathers and mothers of Progressive Education invented. It's the crux of that whole idea of getting kids out from behind their stultifying rows of desks and working on projects, in teams.

The School in Rose Valley, fifteen miles outside of Philadelphia, has a special place both in my heart and in the annals of Progressive Education. Founded in 1929 by parents who came to the Valley to join the local arts and crafts community and who also favored John Dewey's approach to education over the reigning factory model, it is one of the handful of progressive schools that have kept their doors open through most of the last century. Through all these years, it has preserved some of our movement's best traditions, including the central place of the woodshop. As its former principal Grace Rotzel explained, in her book *The School in Rose Valley,* the shop was the first classroom to be built. It has ever since remained integral to the school, out of respect for its power to help build character. Rotzel wrote that:

> *Working with tools furnishes one of the best disciplines a school can offer. Up to this point in a child's life, his discipline has come almost always from some person emotionally close to him. With things like tools, he is free to impose his own discipline. He wants the result, or frequently, in a very young child, he merely wants the satisfaction of the act of sawing and hammering. In any case, the desire to make things is so general in children that they are willing to go through much hard work to reach their ends. This is discipline.*

In her history of the school, Rotzel described how shop class students as young as ten years old helped build the walls and foundation for an extension to a classroom building. When their teacher told them it was time to move on to another project, the students protested loudly that they wanted to keep going and dig the trenches for the plumbing.

On my 2013 visit to the school, which sits on 8.5 wooded acres with sheep and chickens grazing outside the classrooms, I found pre-K through sixth-grade students taking on similarly "adult" projects with confidence. All of the children use full-sized tools, since—as the school's Web site notes—only full-sized tools are strong enough to perform real work. Using real tools not only helps develop children's muscle strength and stamina; it contributes to building character, as students rely on each other to work with an awareness of one another's safety and to clean up and put things back in their place after each project.

The children are allowed to make anything they want, other

than weapons. Recent projects that students have made and taken home include go-carts, desks, chairs, lemonade stands, and a chicken coop. Kids can also work with electronics and appliances at a "tinker table," where they learn the fundamentals of circuitry, and have made battery-powered flashlights and motorized toys.

I wish I could tell you that this sort of scene is common at all of our progressive schools, but the sad truth is that it isn't. Free as so many of us are from the pressures of standardized tests, too many of us still shy away from having students dedicate the time and ambition needed for extensive construction projects. Alas, woodshop classes like Rose Valley still has today are a rarity, even in progressive schools, even as we're much more prone to tinker, invent, and create than the vast majority of conventional schools, an attitude we bring not only to arts projects but to high-technology pursuits.

John Chubb, president of the National Association of Independent Schools, captured this mind-set in his description of the Idea Lab at the Hillbrook School, a private school for pre-schoolers to eighth-graders, founded in 1935, and set in the foothills of Santa Cruz, California. The iLab, as it's known, is a center of "blended" learning—meaning students can learn online, with iPads and laptops, as well as via books, peers, and teachers. It occupies an old computer lab that was refitted with mounted and mobile whiteboards, mobile furniture, a professional soundbooth, robotics kits, and multimedia devices. The school, which is documenting how the lab affects learning, compares its program to similar spaces used by top universities and such Silicon Valley titans as Facebook, Google, Apple, and Cisco, and claims it is one of the first elementary schools to build such a space for students.

As Chubb wrote in a blog, the room can seem haphazard

and even chaotic, with students forming teams, setting up furniture, and turning to devices as they wish. The guiding principle is student choice, allowing kids a precious sense of control over their own education. The whole point, as Chubb noted, is that "Students must ultimately leave school fully capable of learning on their own, and motivated to do so for a lifetime."

At the Galloway School, Mark Gerl is an eloquent advocate for the efficacy of making learning joyful—and addictive—with the lure of modern technology. He tells of a student who was giving him a virtual tour of the popular game "World of Warcraft." As Gerl recalls, "This brilliant seventeen-year-old said, 'They reward curiosity by giving you more things to explore.'" And I said, 'John Francis, do you realize you've just encapsulated everything that's right about education in ten words?'"

CHAPTER 6

Tasting the Soup
Recipes to Calm a "Testing Mania"

Park Day schoolteachers meet with a third-grader.   Photograph by John Orbon

Any school system in which one child may fail while another succeeds is unjust, undemocratic, uneducational.

—MARIETTA JOHNSON (1864–1938), founder of the School of
Organic Education in Fairhope, Alabama

REVOLUTIONARIES IN THE CRYSTAL BALLROOM

On a chilly autumn morning in 2013, my wife Elizabeth has pushed my wheelchair to a front table in the crowded Crystal Ballroom of the Los Angeles Biltmore Hotel.

It's the first day of the fourth national convention of the Progressive Education Network, the association I helped revive starting back in 2005. It's also the first time most of my colleagues have seen me since my cancer diagnosis two months earlier. At each break in the meeting, friends I haven't seen for years come over to hug me, pat my arm, and sometimes, awkwardly, kneel by my knees.

The wheelchair and the awkwardness aside, I'm feeling buoyed this morning—thrilled by the record attendance and the sense of expectation in the room. More than nine hundred teachers and heads of schools from as far away as Canada, Russia, and Japan have convened here, encouraging my growing sense that our movement is poised for an international resurgence.

That the Biltmore opened in 1923, the heyday of Progressive Education, makes it a serendipitous setting for our network's largest convention to date. Even so, the decor, a mix of Beaux-Arts and Renaissance Revival—with giant chandeliers, floor-to-ceiling gold mirrors, and stained-glass windows—may be a little snooty for the majority of our members, who are scraping by on teachers' salaries, and have come to hear speakers including the legendary leftists turned education reformers William Ayers and Angela Davis. Some of our attendees are staying in less expensive hotels a few blocks away, their faces still flushed from the early morning walk. Or maybe that's merely a sign of the emotion evoked by this morning's keynote speaker, the San Francisco Bay Area therapist Madeline Levine, author of The Price of Privilege: How Parental Pressure and Material Advantage Are Creating a Generation of Disconnected and Unhappy Kids (2008). *Levine is delivering a potent reminder of just how much is at stake in our struggle for more humane schools.*

Levine's books detail the misery of recent generations of overpressured children, and today she begins with a list of alarming signposts of American youth's declining mental health, ticking off statistics about mental disorders, substance abuse, and what seems to be increasing cynicism. We're familiar with the numbers from reading the daily newspapers. One in four U.S. high school students will have an episode of major depression. About 17 percent of high school students are drinking, using drugs, or smoking during the school day. More than 80 percent of students have cheated on tests by the time they leave high school.

Most hauntingly, suicide continues to be the third leading cause of death among young people (and the second leading cause of death in college-aged youth). Just a few years ago, in the privileged community of Palo Alto, California, the heart of hard-charging Silicon Valley, four teens within six months killed themselves by standing in front of oncoming trains.

In the past, adolescents have told pollsters that their leading sources of stress were relationships with family and friends. These days, Levine informs us, they more often cite tests and homework: the frantic competition to make the next deadline, ace the next exam, and pump up that college application. "This current paradigm of drills, and testing, and where-are-you-going-to-school—it's killing kids," she says.

All of us here in the Crystal Ballroom know what she's talking about. Over the years, we've watched the rise in students' stress levels. The reasons are complicated, including seemingly justified fears about a dwindling future job market and generalized information overload from our omnipresent computerized devices. What's foremost in our minds this morning, however, is the acute recent increase in high-stakes, government-mandated standardized tests, which for many children now begin as early as first grade. The resulting pressure on public schools and even many private schools to "teach to the test," substituting rote memorization for meaningful learning, has dramatically reduced time for art, music, independent projects, and even lunch. Kids at some schools have complained they get barely fifteen minutes to gobble down their food and return to their desks.

Progressive educators are among the most fervent conscientious objectors to these developments. Our efforts to preserve our schools as islands of sanity are part of our long-lived heritage as educational revolutionaries. As early as 1919, one of the movement's founding fathers, Carleton Washburne, famously dispensed with formal grades in favor of "goal cards," which tracked each student's progress against his or her own goals. Washburne favored "individualized learning," allowing each student to pursue work at his or her own pace, "unhurried by those who are quicker and unhampered by those who are slower." The differences among children in a single classroom were usually great, he noted, adding: "Any form of grading that shames the child who is less able or less mature in any aspect of this work than another member of the class is unfair and discouraging, and takes away his sense of security. Each child must be praised in terms of how well he achieves goals that are within his reach."

I can only imagine what Washburne would think of today's battery of high-stakes tests, as well as the increasing pressures to inflate GPAs and pile on extracurricular achievements. Yet I suspect he would have been proud of our modern progressive schools. Many of us ban standardized tests altogether, and many, as Washburne did, reject letter grades. We believe this sort of competition brings out the worst in students, making them grub for extrinsic rewards rather than develop intrinsic virtues such as curiosity and compassion.

When it's my turn to stand at the podium—and I'm grateful that I can still stand, at least for a few moments at a time—I talk briefly about John Dewey and Carleton Washburne and the first meeting of the Progressive Education Association, nearly a century ago. I tell my colleagues about my recent travels to progressive schools throughout the *country, and of the handy three-part definition I brought home with me. I turn then to acknowledge that many of today's educators are ambivalent about calling themselves "progressive." Even so, I say, now is the time to proudly reclaim that word and our heritage.*

Today we are more relevant than ever.

FAILING GRADES FOR THE "ACCOUNTABILITY" MOVEMENT

In the year leading up to our conference at the Biltmore, I've been delighted to watch a popular backlash building against an educational "accountability" movement that has robbed students of opportunities for meaningful and lasting learning—not to mention a decent lunch hour. In 2013, teachers at six Seattle high schools refused to administer a new standardized test they said was useless. Students in sixteen states boycotted standardized tests based on the new Common Core curriculum. And the New York State United Teachers' union demanded a three-year moratorium on high-stakes testing. In the midst of all this, a movement calling itself the Badass Teachers Association (BAT) and claiming 20,000 members announced its support for "every teacher who refuses to be blamed for the failure of our society to erase poverty and inequality, and refuses to accept assessments, tests, and evaluations imposed by those who have contempt for real teaching and learning." Whipping up the anti-test fervor even more over the past four years have been thousands of screenings, at schools throughout the nation, of the 2009 documentary *Race to Nowhere: The Dark Side of America's Achievement Culture,* which features stories of hard-driven students with stress-related illnesses—including that of a perfectionist thirteen-year-old girl who committed suicide.

The *New York Times* has denounced America's "testing mania." From the Bush administration's No Child Left Behind law in 2001 through the Obama administration's 2009 Race to the Top initiative, federal, state, and local officials have demanded that schools demonstrate success with results on standardized tests. But many educators protest that today's tests are so poorly designed and developmentally inappropriate that they are making students fear and hate going to school.

In late 2013, Carol Burris, an award-winning New York City high school principal, wrote a scathing review of a test for first-graders, focusing on a question that offered four choices to a problem asking, "Which is a related subtraction sentence?" Burris noted that her nephew's wife, who teaches calculus, was stumped by the wording. On her blog, she posted a copy of the test, which had been given to her by a distraught mother. The woman's son, after dutifully answering the first several questions, had collapsed toward the end into writing big awkward "X's" through the problems, clearly giving up hope of answering them correctly.

Now, we progressive educators have no objections to accountability, per se. Scientists have shown that the occasional test can help students learn. It's also clear to us that some teachers, schools, and even states truly ought to be held to higher standards. Yet we're convinced that our national testing mania is doing more harm than good. We're also dismayed by increasing evidence that the nationwide increase in standardized tests has done the most harm to minority and low-income students, widening the income equality gap. And we question some of the motives driving the trend.

In recent years, educational testing has become a multibillion-dollar industry, driven by big international corporations such as Pearson and Educational Testing Services. Simultaneously, both the number and frequency of standardized tests have been ratcheting up, as many school districts have been adding their own tests to prepare students for the federally mandated ones. Today's college-bound students find themselves undergoing a continuous stream of these high-pressure tests, including not only the mandated exams to track schools' progress but SSATs (for private school applicants), PSATs, SATs, ACTs, and four-hour-long Advanced Placement tests, on top of the usual bevy of spot quizzes, mid-terms, and finals.

New laws in many states have tied teachers' salaries and even jobs to students' scores. As a result, what used to be a thoughtful, creative profession has become more like working in a factory. Educators are told: Here is the text. This is what we want you to teach; this is how long you can spend teaching it; and this is how we'll judge your performance. For students, the changes are making many of today's classrooms seem ever more like the harsh, boring schoolrooms of the early twentieth century.

In my more than a hundred hours of conversations with progressive teachers and principals over the past year, I've heard a rise in anxiety that many of us now share with our colleagues in conventional schools.

The worries are worst for teachers in progressive public schools, which in most cases must abide by district policy. In early 2014, Chris Collaros, principal of the Wickliffe Elementary School, said new Ohio State laws ranking teachers according to test results were not only making it harder for the school to retain its progressive identity but undermining teachers' effectiveness. "I have to put teachers in a box, based on a rubric with ten different elements of teaching," he said. "That shuts down a lot of good conversation and makes progressive innovating a lot harder to do. It's a one-size-fits-all model."

As director of the independent K–6 Children's Community School in Van Nuys, California, Neal Wrightson is relatively immune from such pressures, but worries that for children in mainstream schools, the value system being taught is "I'm good at this. Too bad for you," rather than "I'm good at this. Let me help you."

The test-driven return to rote learning may be hurting our economy as well as our society, by squelching signs of idiosyncratic creativity and leadership, the very qualities we need to keep our GNP growing. Instead, most current assessments track only the most low-level, easily measured thinking.

To be sure, even Park Day School hasn't been entirely exempt from some forms of rote learning. I'll give you a small example, a pet peeve of mine. I have yet to find a ten-year-old who can truly understand, much less explain, the concept of dividing fractions. Even adults often have a hard time with this level of abstraction. Nonetheless, a typical problem on a fifth-grade math test, and, of course, many of the standardized tests, is: "How many two-thirds are there in seven-ninths?" To answer this problem, fifth-graders have traditionally learned a simple trick: invert and multiply. This means they can mindlessly "solve" the problem when they see it—but is this really how we create future scientists and engineers? Still, we teach this trick at Park Day, and have done so for years, because not to do so would be to leave our students unprepared in high school or beyond, when they eventually will have to take a standardized test.

Skeptical as we are about the worth of standardized assessments, it bears noting that U.S. students' scores on the international PISA exams haven't appreciably improved over the past decade. More significantly, all this testing doesn't appear to be helping prepare kids for college. A 2012 study showed

Americans complete college at lower than average rates among countries tracked by the Organization for Economic Cooperation and Development (OECD). With nearly half of U.S. college students dropping out before they get a degree, we rank behind Japan and Finland, as well as Hungary, Chile, and Italy. The skyrocketing expense of going to college is surely a factor for the dropouts—the cost has nearly sextupled since 1985—but so, say many experts, are abysmal levels of student preparedness.

All this said, for many teachers and parents alike, not to mention school district officials, the concreteness of the standardized test scores and GPAs are hard to resist. Such metrics, after all, are much easier to track than descriptors of children's mental health. Indeed, throughout the country, newspapers publish schools' test results, which realtors use to attract buyers into supposedly high-achieving neighborhoods.

This makes it all the more meaningful when prominent parents stand up to the mania, which is why I'm intrigued to hear some buzz at the PEN Conference concerning the Oscar-winning film star Matt Damon. In an interview with the British newspaper *The Guardian* just a few days before our conference opened, Damon said that after a "giant family discussion" he had decided to enroll his four children in a progressive private school in Los Angeles. He would rather have sent them to public school, he said, but the kind of progressive education he himself had enjoyed as a public school student "no longer exists in the public system."

In a follow-up piece in *Time* magazine, Los Angeles School District superintendent John Deasy contended that there were indeed progressive options in his district, and that he would be happy to help Damon find one. Still, Deasy and Damon weren't all that far apart. In a subsequent interview for this book, Deasy acknowledged that American schools are suffering from a shortage of "thoughtful, rigorous assessments" combined with "far too many discrete high-stakes tests—and they are not serving students."

Happily, some progressive public schools are managing to buck the system, or at least parts of it. The Winnetka School District doesn't give any letter grades until seventh grade, substituting narrative reports. At Mission Hill School in Boston, Ayla Gavins has gone further, firmly resisting almost all of the battery of district-mandated standardized assessments, even though she fears it has alienated school district officials.

Gavins is obliged to allow at least one standardized state test a year in order for her school to receive government funding under the No Child Left Behind law. But she told me she has held the line against other district-mandated tests, designed to help students do better on the federally mandated ones:

The materials are sent to my school and sit there, and then I get a phone call that says, we have not gotten your testing results; the window is going to close, and I say, thanks very much, but it's not coming. Then I get a phone call from someone higher up saying this testing is mandated, and I say, yes, I got that, and I'm also trying to speak with the superintendent on this issue, thank you very much. I'm not silently boycotting; I've been forward and open about that this just isn't happening. I'm pushing back because I don't think it benefits our students, don't think it offers information better than what teachers are getting in real time, and don't think it's a good use of anyone's time.

Gavins's unusual national prestige—linked to her school's extraordinary success—may have helped spare her from sanctions for this rebellion. Her school, a model of the best of progressive traditions, has been the star of a documentary film, *A*

Year at Mission Hill, and the subject of a book, *Democratic Education in Practice: Inside the Mission Hill School,* by Matthew Knoester, an assistant professor of education at the University of Evansville. Knoester points out the school's accomplishments, including the fact that more than 96 percent of the graduates surveyed have gone on to college. Moreover, local families are flocking to Mission Hill; each year, Gavins must turn away about two thirds of the children who apply because she refuses to compromise on the policy of small student-teacher ratios. All this could explain why, instead of being disciplined for her conscientious objecting, Gavins has been invited to join district-level committees investigating ways to allow schools more self-determination.

As parents, teachers, and brave public school principals were standing up to the standardized tests in 2013, even Arne Duncan acknowledged they had some justification. At a May 2013 meeting of the American Educational Research Association, the education secretary said that much of the criticism of the tests was merited, and that the tests had some serious flaws. He went on to argue that the solution to mediocre tests isn't to abandon assessment but to support *better* assessment.

I was happy to hear that.

Because better forms of assessment already exist. We practice them at progressive schools every day.

SOS FOR TEST-STRESSED KIDS

Let's be frank: "accountability" and assessments are touchy subjects for many progressive educators, for good reason. Even some of our friendliest critics sometimes confuse our strategy of considering children's emotional welfare in deciding how and what we teach as a lack of "rigor." (The popular progressive educator Alfie Kohn aptly responds that the alternative is more like "rigor mortis.") Or they judge the whole movement on the basis of the few schools that haven't held true to Progressive Education's traditional standards, which in point of fact are plenty rigorous.

Take Harvard's Tony Wagner, one of today's most-quoted education gurus. Wagner is a pioneer of the "21st Century Learning" movement, which he acknowledged, in an interview for this book, has strong roots in Progressive Education. "The ideas of learning by doing, of more emphasis on skills as opposed to content, of more hands-on tasks, and of a focus on student motivation—that's all in the best of progressive tradition," he said. Yet he went on to argue that the main difference between Progressive Education and 21st Century Learning lies in what he described as a general resistance to being held to standard measures of accountability. "This has always been the movement's Achilles' Heel," he said.

The truth, as always, is more complicated. Our best progressive schools unquestionably hold students accountable. The difference is that we evaluate learning progress with more nuanced, thorough, and telling techniques than having children fill in bubbles on a form. These include mastering standards that let kids keep trying until they get it right, and an emphasis on continual self-assessment.

My colleague and friend Scott Duyan, head of school at the private, pre-K–8 Presidio Hill School in San Francisco, the oldest continuously operating progressive school west of the Mississippi, compares this to a chef tasting his soup before serving it to customers. It relays the message that students must assume responsibility for their own learning, strengthening a skill that could—and should—last a lifetime.

In 2004, Duyan and I went to bat for our beliefs, successfully challenging the California Association of Independent Schools (CAIS) requirement that its members administer a standardized test with the ungainly title of ERB CTP 4. (Independent schools are free to opt out of federally mandated tests, but many administer the Comprehensive Testing Program, administered by the global, non-profit Educational Records Bureau, to guarantee standardized achievement.) Up until then, our two schools' determined rejection of such tests had deprived us of accreditation essential to our ability to network with other independent schools. Our first attempt to change the rule failed, but we strengthened our case with a binder full of research about why standardized tests aren't adequate measurements of learning, and why our alternatives work better. Over the next five years, other educators joined us, until finally the CAIS ruled in our favor, noting what it called a growing sentiment that mandating standardized assessments "had the unintended consequence of having schools focus more upon administering the test, rather than upon developing assessment philosophies, tools, and practices."

Our thoughts, precisely.

Over the past century, progressive schools have put a lot of effort and attention into developing effective alternative forms of assessment. Instead of the one-size-fits-all standardized exam or the Friday morning spot quiz, we have always favored the sorts of evaluations supported by research and described in the landmark National Research Council report *How People Learn*, as those that "provide students with opportunities to revise and improve their thinking, help students see their own progress over the course of weeks or months, and help teachers identify problems that need to be remedied."

Our leading alternatives include student presentations and

portfolios; teachers' thoughtfully individualized accounts of students' academic and social development; and student-led conferences with teachers and parents that help students think more deeply about how they are progressing.

Now I'll tell you how this all works at Park Day School, which, I'll grant you, is exceptional even among progressive schools for the extraordinary amount of time and effort we devote to assessing students in what we believe are truly meaningful ways, and of communicating their progress to parents. Even as we spare our students from letter grades or standardized tests, we are *rigorous* when it comes to our assessments.

Twice a year, every Park Day School teacher writes a report for each of their students, typically amounting to from fourteen to eighteen pages. In each grade level, students and their families receive feedback (often including detailed comments) as to whether they are meeting, not meeting, or exceeding expectations in literally dozens of categories, based on state requirements and an in-school consensus on developmental expectations. In the first grade, for instance, rather than simply be rated in progress for Mathematics, English, and Art, as they would in conventional schools, students are evaluated in fourteen separate categories under Social/Emotional progress (including "demonstrates impulse control," "solves conflicts constructively," "accepts responsibility for actions"), and twenty-two categories under Approach to Learning, Work, and Play (including "is punctual," "demonstrates curiosity and enthusiasm for learning," "completes assignments in a timely way," and "engages in imaginative play"), before the reports even mention progress in Language Arts (thirty categories, including "reads long vowel words," "reads short vowel words," "stays on the topic when speaking," and "reads with expression"), Mathematics (nineteen categories, including "counts by 2s, 5s, 10s," "recognizes and extends patterns," and "classifies objects by common attributes"), and Science (nine categories, including, "asks relevant questions" and "participates in group discussions.")

Kindergarten, first-, and second-grade students are rated in each category as "developing," "often" (i.e., excelling), "consistent," or "area of concern," with areas of concern always thoroughly explained. Children at later grade levels get even more extensive comments.

Karen Colaric, the lower school director, says it takes her forty hours during each assessment period to review all the reports. "Teachers from other schools are consistently amazed at how much detail we go into and how honest we are," she says. And, yes, Park Day teachers have occasionally been known to complain about the workload.

Over the years, the great majority of our students have gone on from Park Day to mainstream high schools, where they've had to accommodate to more conventional practices. Acknowledging this, we instituted a test-taking course for middle-schoolers, to make sure they leave Park Day equipped to cope with America's testing mania.

While Park Day School is surely an outlier in both our determined ban on standardized tests and grades and our painstaking approach to assessment, you'd be mistaken to think that other private schools and even public schools couldn't follow our model. Many already do. Consider Casco Bay High School in Portland, Maine, named one of Maine's top schools by *U.S. News & World Report*. The school uses a "standards-based" grading system, based on its students' mastery of specific skills and concepts derived from Maine's state standards and the new Common Core, combined with ratings of participation and effort. Each high school course is built around ten to fifteen standards, describing concepts and skills that students are expected to learn and achieve. The school formally outlines progress ten times a year through detailed report cards, progress reports, and conferences, in addition to which an online gradebook is updated frequently.

Rather than receive letter grades, students are told that they either are failing to meet school standards, approaching the standards, very close to meeting the standards, meeting the standards, or exceeding the standards. They get many different opportunities to show what they know and can do, and are expected to build a body of work to demonstrate mastery of each course standard. In contrast with common practice, if students show they are working hard, they get extra time after the term has ended to meet the standards.

At the Wickliffe Elementary School in Ohio, grading also significantly varies from the norm. Report cards include sections on Community, Compassion, and Civility, and rather than separate grades for science and social studies, there's a section for Thematic Units of Study, demonstrating the school's commitment to interdisciplinary learning. Much like at Park Day School, albeit in considerably less detail, students are regularly assessed on their progress in learning to respect the rights and feelings of others, accept responsibility for their behavior, and solve problems appropriately.

I've talked with many students who have deep appreciation for schools that are willing to work on alternatives to the rigid prevailing norm.

"I have friends at other schools who are studying for finals right now, and they're really stressed out," said Austin Wilson, a high school junior enrolled at the Wildwood School, a private, progressive K–12 school in Los Angeles. Wilson, who spoke on a panel at the PEN Conference in Los Angeles, transferred to Wildwood from a private Catholic school when he was in eighth grade. Now, he says, when he talks to his old friends from other schools, he hears a lot about students resorting to taking ADHD stimulant medications such as Ritalin or Adderall to get them through their schoolwork and tests. Abuse of pharmaceutical stimulants as study aides has in fact reached crisis proportions at many high schools throughout the country. Yet Wilson said stimulant abuse is simply not an issue at Wildwood.

Wilson is a serious student with serious goals; he has set his sights on the University of Chicago, where he hopes to major in economics. He and his parents are confident that Wildwood has prepared him well. "The way we learn at school has made me more reflective, instead of just spitting out data on a test," he said. The school's regular but non-traditional assessments of its students take into account not only mastery of content but "Habits of Heart and Mind," which include critical thinking, collaboration, being able to look at issues from multiple perspectives, and ethical behavior.

Wilson said he wasn't worried that colleges to which he might apply would have trouble understanding his transcript, saying the school provided an equation to translate its unusual assessments into grades and GPAs to satisfy college admissions boards. At the same time, he said, the more detailed assessments have helped him know which specific skills he needed to improve. "In the end, it's quite close to traditional grading, but the students get a deeper understanding of their progress," he said.

Abby Lee, another junior at Wildwood, acknowledged that sometimes this sort of assessment makes students unsure about how they would fare in a traditional grading system, but she still shared Wilson's enthusiasm, saying: "Getting an entire paragraph of comments from your teachers about your strengths and 'stretches' is far more helpful than a single letter grade. It lets me know how I'm doing and what I can do better. It not only informs me about my own performance but it also helps me understand how I am as a learner and a person."

METRICS OF THE HEART

I'm encouraged to see an increasing number of mostly private schools not only cultivating but starting to figure out how to assess some hugely important cognitive and emotional skills that until fairly recently haven't been major educational priorities. What I find to be a particularly fascinating development is that since 2009, an expanding group of independent schools have been administering an online "Mission Skills" assessment developed by a non-profit organization called INDEX (for Independent Schools Data Exchange) and the for-profit Educational Testing Services. This unusual test seeks to measure the six character traits of teamwork, creativity, ethics, resilience, curiosity, and time management. To guard against potential biases, each skill is measured three ways. First, students take an hour-long test that both asks for biographical data—such as how many times they pursued some activity in a given month—and tests how students might respond to hypothetical situations. (In one such question, students have been asked what they would do if after they had been working hard on a team project, one member turned in badly written work shortly before the project deadline. The listed choices are: turn in the work and not worry; suggest how the student might improve his or her work; tell the teacher; or rewrite the work for the student.) For each student, a teacher at the school who knows that student well will then fill out an in-depth evaluation.

A RAND Corporation report on measuring twenty-first-century skills gave the Mission Skills test kudos, saying that teachers testify that such assessments help establish a common language that make such skills easier to teach, while indirectly making students feel more valued. At last count, 112 schools were administering the test, including three that I visited on my tour in 2013.

Students' scores on these tests are not divulged in detail to the students or their families. Instead, teachers and administrators use them to better understand how well they are pursuing their stated missions of teaching these twenty-first-century skills, and to try to improve.

LEARNING AT LARGE

On my travels to progressive schools, I repeatedly witnessed scenes that illustrated what so many students trapped in the testing mania are unfortunately losing from our obsession with metrics. I'll share one of these with you now.

At the Wingra private progressive school in Madison, Wisconsin, on a below-freezing day, four first-graders asked to go outside during recess to play in the snow. Their teachers clearly had been hoping they would choose to stay indoors, yet they readily granted permission. And even though, as a Californian unused to the cold, I'd been quite happy to stick close to the radiator, I chose to follow them.

Merely the necessary preparations to leave the classroom required a generous attitude toward time that is sadly in rare supply at most American schools. Consider how long it takes for a six-year-old to pull on snow pants, a jacket, and snow boots, with zippers, buttons, and laces that require advanced fine motor control and eye-hand coordination. And who is to say whether at this point in a child's development, this exercise—engaged in with such calm deliberation—is less important than an equal number of minutes spent on math exercises or reading?

Outside, the children went to work on a two-foot-tall, vaguely humanoid snow sculpture they had begun the day before. As I watched, I became engrossed by one little girl, in a pink sweater and red vest, who was determinedly trying to fashion what looked like a garland for the sculpture, out of ice. She must have made a dozen different attempts during the twenty minutes they were out there. Completely intent on her effort, without a word to her friends, she tried first to make something she could pick up and place on the head of the snow-person, and then, when that didn't work, tried to sculpt on the head, awkwardly breaking off chunks of ice from the project with her mittens.

Not only was this particular little girl working hard; I could see how she was slowly but directly educating herself about the properties of ice and the nature of structure, as one attempt after the other dissolved in a snowy pile. She returned to class without having achieved her goal. Yet something in the expression on her bright pink face told me she was already thinking about what she would do differently the next time she got back out there.

CHAPTER 7

The Laboratory
Messiness and Failure—Progressive Education's Vulnerability and Strength

A second-grade block-building project at Hubbard Woods Elementary School in Winnetka, Illinois.   Photograph by Kate McLellan

The road to success is through constant blundering.

—COLONEL FRANCIS W. PARKER

"DO YOU CALL THIS A SCHOOL?"

Caroline Pratt, founder of the City and Country School in Manhattan, took mischievous pleasure in the shock that many visitors expressed at the seeming chaos of her classrooms. Most of them had never imagined that school could be like this: a rowdy group of sixth-graders would burst into the room, their overalls worn and stained from kneeling on the floor in drama class, sawing wood planks in shop, and throwing pots in art. Noisily pushing aside tables and chairs, they'd slam open locker doors to grab their books, and settle in to work, each one apparently knowing what needed to be done. Often, the only quiet person in the room was the teacher.

As Pratt wrote in her memoir I Learn from Children *(1948), the children's mothers usually seemed the least distressed by such scenes, as most simply enjoyed seeing their children so happily occupied. Yet occasionally, as she recalled, "a father looked jolted, worried; how in that turmoil, would his son ever get ready for Harvard?"*

The sharpest reaction of all, however, came from visiting teachers used to working in conventional classrooms.

"Do you call this a school?" Pratt said they would ask.

FIGHTING AGAINST FORMULA

The story of Progressive Education is one of chaos and invention, messiness and failure, inspired rebels who threw away rulebooks, excesses bordering on irresponsibility, public acclaim, and public condemnation. Our willingness to question convention is one of our greatest gifts to our students. Yet when some of us have taken that quality to extremes, it has cost us dearly in time wasted on detours and squandered goodwill.

Caroline Pratt was one of the movement's boldest and most

inspiring rebels, rarely making a false move herself. Just seventeen years old when she first started teaching, in a one-room schoolhouse in her hometown of Fayetteville, New York, Pratt was impressed by the eagerness she noticed in young children at play, and equally dismayed by how that enthusiasm seemed to dwindle after they spent just a few years in a conventional classroom. She dreamed of a new kind of school that would encourage rather than squelch creativity. "I began to see education not as an end in itself, but as the first step in progress which should continue during a lifetime," she wrote.

After attending Teachers College in New York, Pratt in 1914 established her new school in Greenwich Village, a neighborhood that was just then beginning to attract a stream of writers and artists who welcomed her innovations. She dispensed with set curriculum, formal instruction, and grades for her youngest students. Filling her classrooms with blocks, crayons, paper, and clay, she encouraged children to discover and pursue their interests through play. Later on, she would guide them in reading, writing, and arithmetic, while also taking them on frequent field trips around town to expose them to the world of work.

The City and Country School became one of the most daring educational laboratories of the era, with students and teachers alike constantly testing hypotheses, cheerfully failing, and then trying again. "All my life I have fought against formula," Pratt later wrote. "Once you set down a formula, you are imprisoned by it." As other progressive educators followed similar paths, they developed philosophies and tactics still considered cutting edge today, from appreciation of the role of unstructured play in a child's neurological development to the mastery system of learning, in which students are allowed many attempts, instead of just one, to get something right.

I thought of Pratt and her aversion to blueprints on a recent morning as I was wandering through a toy store, looking for a gift for a young friend. I had planned to buy a set of Legos, but to my frustration couldn't find a box that didn't feature a finely detailed photograph of the final product: a fully constructed pirate's ship, a rocket, or a gas station, all with little Lego figures in their suggested places. It reminded me of how many children today are growing up in a world in which we adults pretend to know all the answers, laying out detailed instructions for them to proceed. While this can make our job as teachers more predictable and easy, it risks robbing students of the self-confidence that comes only after they summon the courage to try and fail and then try again.

This, after all, is an ideal preparation for scientists. As David Brazer, an associate professor at Stanford's Graduate School of Education, reminded me, science is rooted in experimentation. Yet despite the strong U.S. push to get more students engaged in science, there's a deep contradiction in the trend of conventional schools to avoid experimentation in favor of emphasizing the "right" answers on rigid exams of a narrow set of data. "Unless and until communities, schools, districts, and states allow for well-conceived experimentation (and the concomitant risks of failure), we are unlikely to make substantial progress improving overall student performance and narrowing achievement gaps," Brazer said.

The most skillful teachers know how to tolerate the ambiguity of experimentation. They also know when to step back and pretend they're invisible. That's why, whenever I observe in a classroom, I like to measure the ratio of "teacher talk" to "student talk." When the ratio tips toward the students, it often means kids are testing their critical thinking skills. A noisier classroom is much harder to manage, but often more productive.

I worry that today all too many conventional classrooms are

returning to the teaching style that Pratt and her contemporaries found so deadening: with students sitting quietly at desks, fearful of making any sort of mistake, as they listen to teachers assuming the role of the "sage on the stage." In contrast, as Pratt wrote, in *her* school, "nothing was fixed, nothing stayed put, not even the furniture; above all, not the children!" She welcomed the messiness and failure that gave students and teachers alike the opportunity to learn from mistakes.

Now, like all of us, Pratt was a product of her times. As the Progressive Era bloomed into the Jazz Age, something similar to her brand of liberated self-expression and tolerance for trial and error was infusing the world outside her classroom—in art, music, and architecture. Artists including Salvador Dalí, René Magritte, Frank Lloyd Wright, F. Scott Fitzgerald, Eugene O'Neill, and Ernest Hemingway were all boldly challenging convention, in a time that produced more than its share both of enduring masterpieces and quickly forgotten flops. And so it was, too, in many progressive classrooms, as Lawrence Cremin has noted. "License began to pass for liberty, planlessness for spontaneity, recalcitrance for individuality, obfuscation for art, and chaos for education—all justified in the rhetoric of expressionism," he wrote, adding, "and thus was born at least one of the several caricatures of Progressive Education in which humorists reveled—quite understandably—for at least a generation."

For decades to come, these wags would press the point that as classrooms grew more lax, society would pay the price. One classic cartoon shows a long-haired young doctor telling a dismayed-looking older patient, sitting in his underwear: "Well, you see, I went to one of those progressive medical schools with no formal classes or credits and students plan their own course of study so I never learned anything about the lungs, breathing, and all that."

That particular cartoon was drawn in the 1980s, by which time those Americans who feared that progressive reforms would lead to anarchy had a vivid posterboy.

Its name was Summerhill.

FREE-RANGE CHILDHOOD

While it's more than likely that neither John Dewey, Colonel Francis Parker, Caroline Pratt, nor most other American progressive pioneers would ever have approved of Summerhill— the utopian private British boarding school that in 1960 inspired an international best-selling book, subtitled *A New View of Childhood*—it remains one of the most famous "progressive" schools. It is also a major example, to my mind, of taking good ideas too far. Since its founding in 1921, Summerhill has done more than any other school to perpetuate the harmful, largely erroneous caricature that Progressive Education equals pure permissiveness. One writer described it as "free-range childhood."

The school, now located in eastern Suffolk, is most famous for three things: its uncompromising democracy (children have equal votes with adults in determining school rules); students' freedom to decide if they want to attend class or not; and the many outrageous declarations of its firebrand founder, the former Scottish journalist A. S. Neill, who died in 1973.

To critics who charged him with denying children basic education, Neill responded: "To hell with arithmetic." To those who accused him of refusing to "mold" children's characters, he retorted: "No one is wise enough or good enough to mold the character of any child. What is wrong with our sick, neurotic world is that we have been molded, and an adult generation that has seen two great wars and seems about to launch a third should not be trusted to mold the character of a rat."

"Free schools" modeled after Summerhill mushroomed in the United Kingdom and United States during the anti-authoritarian 1970s, but then steadily lost popularity. In 1999, British officials tried to shut Summerhill down, charging it with abrogating its responsibility to educate its students. The school fought back in court and won. In recent years it has attracted about half of its pupils from overseas, many of them from East Asia, sent by parents who feel that their own local schools are too oppressive. (There's even a Summerhill International School in Tokyo.) Loosely modeled after Summerhill, meanwhile, is a global network of a couple dozen so-called Sudbury schools, including several in the United States. Originating from the first Sudbury Valley School, founded in 1968 in Framingham, Massachusetts, they're distinguished by their lack of curriculum; students study only what they wish to learn. Children of all ages mix together; parents have limited involvement; and students and staff run their schools as democracies where everyone has an equal vote.

I never came across any record of Dewey commenting on specific schools, much less Summerhill. Still, it's easy to guess what he might have said. By the late 1920s, without naming names, he was worrying publicly about the movement's most dogmatic members, complaining that "They conceive of no alternative to adult dictation save child dictation." Later, in his classic *Experience and Education*, Dewey fretted that some progressive educators were wrongly trying to eliminate organized subject matter altogether, focusing on the present and future, as he described it, to the exclusion of the past.

I doubt that Dewey ever came close to considering that children should be able to choose whether or not they show up for class, and, for the record, neither have I. Both before and after Dewey, mainstream progressive educators—if that's not too much of an oxymoron—have always sought to balance efforts to tend to a student's cognitive and emotional needs. And from where I sit, giving a young person absolute freedom to say yes or no to school addresses neither of these needs. While I do believe that young children and teens need more control over their lives and their learning than they have in conventional schools, they just as certainly need some structure and guidance from adults.

ADJUSTMENT PROBLEMS

Dewey's worry in 1938 about progressive schools going to unreasonable extremes unfortunately proved prescient. Within a decade, the reformers, by many accounts, sapped their remaining popularity with their overly enthusiastic embrace of the "life-adjustment" movement: the idea that schools should start providing students with a lot more social guidance.

The notion formally arose in a 1945 report by the Department of Education, whose authors said that 60 percent of high school students required more attention from schools to their "physical, mental, and emotional health," their "present problems of youth," and their "preparation for future living." This wasn't at all a bad idea: high school students—especially those not bound for college—truly needed practical advice in navigating such challenges as getting a job and maintaining a relationship.

Yet for many conservative critics in an increasingly conformist postwar culture, the new "life-adjustment" curriculum threatened the last bastion of a classic liberal education. They reasonably feared that as schools spent more time teaching physical fitness, nutrition, and dating skills, there would be less time for geometry, physics, Latin, and American history.

The prominent education expert Diane Ravitch, in her history of American education, *The Troubled Crusade,* describes how the life-adjustment fad reached such a pitch that at one junior high school in Tulsa, Oklahoma, all traditional subject matter— English, science, math, and history—was merged into a single core class, called "Social Relations," with students spending the rest of the day in shop, in the laboratory, or on the playground. Students in a high school in Oakland, California, meanwhile, took courses for credit in "Leisure Activities" or "Personal Management." Growing public skepticism about these trends contributed to an eventual popular retreat from progressive schools.

Even so, despite its controversial history, the life-adjustment movement has maintained a surprisingly strong influence in modern public schools, which continue to teach kids about proper diets and sex education, while also providing counseling on finding internships and jobs. I think that's as it should be: as de facto community leaders, schools can and must use their unique resources to help guide children in decisions that will strongly affect their lives, especially when so many parents lack the time and capacity to do so. While working on this book, I was pleased to hear of a recent addition to this trend: a new, school-based program sponsored by the Centers for Disease Control and Prevention to help prevent dating violence among teens. Acting on evidence that as many as one in four adolescents experiences some sort of dating violence, which inevitably becomes more dangerous over time, the CDC developed a five-year pilot educational program focusing on eleven- to fourteen-year-olds in high-risk parts of Baltimore, Chicago, Fort Lauderdale, and our own hometown of Oakland. I'd argue that such programs are a credit to the life-adjustment movement, maligned as it was.

At the same time this episode taught progressive educators what should be an unforgettable lesson about the value of moderation. It wasn't the only time we've had to head back to the chalkboard, and of course it won't be the last.

THREE PROGRESSIVE PITFALLS

As a student, teacher, and head of school, I've always valued mistakes as a pathway to learning. Mistakes have continually improved my life and my teaching, and I have no doubt that mistakes have helped strengthen education reform.

That said, I believe there are three main mistakes we progressive educators have made that are worth summarizing here, since they've contributed so much to the stigma we need to confront and change. All boil down to excesses: in the degree of freedom that some of our schools have given children; in the degree of autonomy that some of us have granted teachers; and in the degree to which some of us have lowered our expectations for children's academic performance in favor of attending to what we interpret as their emotional needs.

It's all a matter of balance.

Each excess has arisen from a move in the right direction. Each mistake is the flipside of a major contribution.

Allowing children too much freedom, for instance, is a mistake shared by many well-meaning families and well-meaning schools. Many of us have been reacting against our past experience with over-autocratic parents and educational systems. Still, the most effective schools and families know to provide a mix of love and structure, with the understanding that children need an environment in which they can feel physically and emotionally secure—and consequently free to grow and to learn. At the same time, as progressive educators have recognized for more than a century, without the freedom to make mistakes, children grow up stunted.

At the Putney School, Emily Jones, the principal, described a philosophy that struck me as a good goal for all of us. "We allow things to be messy," she said, adding: "We don't have the expectation that every day will be a 'good day.' The kids learn to pick up the pieces and move on; things don't always work out the way we like. We have a well-developed, highly functional safety net, but it is about a foot under their feet. It's not wrapped around them like a cocoon. The place is designed so that adults don't tell the students what to do. Every student has a different schedule; there are no bells. Kids need to find out how to fit it all in. They discover how to run their own lives—in an enormously safe and supportive environment."

Let's now consider the second common excess: that of granting teachers too much autonomy, without a corresponding demand for accountability and teamwork.

Throughout our history, progressive educators have favored an exceptional degree of decision-making power for teachers, believing it contributes to more creativity in the classrooms. Progressive schools are usually run more democratically than most, meaning teachers feel more free to challenge heads of schools when disagreements arise. Because of the exceptional trust that progressive schools place in teachers, we've drawn many more independent-minded folk, including more men. Yet the corresponding risk is that while many teachers (and their students) flourish in a system based on shared decision making, it's not right for every personality. Progressive teachers must also be unusually flexible, in order to collaborate effectively; otherwise, persistent conflicts among teachers erode the strong communities that help students thrive. Progressive school administrators therefore need first to be particularly vigilant about the kinds of teachers we hire, seeking equal parts passion and discipline; and after that, we must work to support strong relationships, steering teachers through inevitable conflicts.

This brings us to our movement's third classic excess: of sometimes failing to hold ourselves and our students to high standards, and especially of overemphasizing students' perceived emotional needs at the expense of cognitive and academic development. This is the origin of the stigma that progressive schools are too lax, and "loosey-goosey." If we truly do want to learn from our mistakes, as we're coaching our students to do, we need to be the first in assessing, criticizing, and remedying our own performance.

From my many conversations with principals and teachers, I know this is a major concern, and that many educators are working hard both to make sure we are sufficiently "rigorous" and that we improve in our ability to communicate with parents who are worried that we aren't. "We need to reveal the purposefulness that exists in our classrooms, and how we draw students into deeper learning," said Michèle Solá, director of the Manhattan Country School. "We are not sloppy; there is order and routine, and a clear methodology." Solá and others reminded me that our obligation to teach content should never come at the expense of helping students build their critical thinking skills. Once again, as always, it's a balancing act.

THE NEURODIVERSITY HURDLE

The Berkeley Parents Network, an active local Web site, attests to Park Day School's loyal following. It's packed with comments from parents extolling the school, with adjectives such as "amazing" and "fantastic" and "phenomenal." One parent says she LOVES us, in capital letters. Another compares the experience of having a daughter attend Park Day to winning one of Willy Wonka's golden tickets. Still another describes us as "social and emotional mentoring intertwined with a top-notch-get-into-Stanford classroom education." The glaring exception to this torrent of praise is a comment that has been on the site since February 2011, and which still makes me wince when I read it. It's from a parent of a son who was diagnosed with ADHD, anxiety, and depression, and who writes about the family's struggles to keep the boy enrolled at Park Day—with the aid of expensive tutors, therapists, and a "shadow teacher," who would sit next to him in class to help him keep up—only to learn that these services might have been provided free of charge had they enrolled their son in public school.

Progressive schools take justified pride in having steadily increased our enrollment of students from diverse ethnic and socioeconomic origins. Alas, we've historically found it harder to integrate children with serious learning and behavioral differences, which for me is a major example of "messiness and failure" that has pushed us to innovate and improve over the years.

To be sure, not all schools are a perfect fit for all children, and even though progressive schools pride ourselves on our strong, accepting communities, the degree of freedom that we allow students can make it especially hard to accommodate children with exceptionally poor impulse control. For much of our history, many progressive private schools have resorted to "counseling out" such challenging children—the standard euphemism for telling families to look elsewhere. We've felt we've had to do this despite our awareness that the families have likely already tried and failed to find a suitable school, have been drawn to the private, progressive school by the small classes and seemingly welcoming environment, and have prepared to make great financial sacrifices to support their child. We've also been aware that there are indeed few good alternatives. Even today, it's rare to find a public or private school that's truly skilled at bringing out the best in children with major learning and behavioral problems. It's true that public schools, as opposed to independent schools, are under legal obligation to provide extra tutoring and other supports once a need for them has been established. Still, they cannot guarantee that the child will be welcomed by his or her peers, or will ever be able to adjust to a mainstream classroom.

On the other hand, our national educational system has come a long way in recent years in better understanding learning and behavioral differences, and in developing ways to help the greatest variety of children get the most out of school without their continually disrupting class for others. I'm happy to report that we have made similar progress at Park Day.

We began to make this progress a priority in 1998, when we hired our first full-time learning specialist—Ilya Pratt, who had previously worked at Park Day as an after-school and substitute teacher, before getting her master's degree in special education. Over the next few years, Pratt oversaw the expansion of a team that by 2014 included two additional specially trained faculty members devoted to supporting students with learning differences. The three specialists routinely conduct individual screenings and informal assessments and provide referrals to specialists and other resources. Beyond that, they also help educate parents and other teachers at the school about a range of learning and behavioral differences. Park Day School was the first independent school in the East Bay Area to run a parent support group for families with children with special needs.

All of our classrooms are now equipped with tools to help

restless, impulsive kids dissipate excess energy without disrupting the class. These include fitness balls to sit on instead of hard chairs, and "fidgets"—little gizmos that distracted kids can play with, like squeeze-balls, or rubber bands fastened around the chair legs, to occupy stray fingers and limbs. As a special project a few years ago, one of our fourth-grade classes manufactured a large set of wooden "T-stools," which are just what they sound like: stools shaped like a large T. The students sitting atop the T must keep moving, if subtly, so as not to lose balance, an exercise that helps many of them stay focused when they have to sit and listen. The fourth-graders, under the skillful direction of their teacher, Bob Rollins, did all the designing, planning, sawing, and decorating of the stools themselves, simultaneously learning about carpentry and the workings of different kinds of brains.

Parents of children who've failed to thrive at other schools continue to seek us out—now more than ever. By 2014, nearly one third of our students had been diagnosed with mild to moderate disabilities, including dyslexia, ADHD, and autism spectrum disorders. While we still aren't the best fit for children with severe impediments, we've greatly expanded the range of kids who can benefit from our school.

"When we are at our best, we are addressing learning differences as we would any other aspect of diversity," says Pratt. "Everybody learns differently. So each student is able to discover what he or she needs to do the best work."

FAIL BETTER

By honestly facing our inevitable mistakes and finding ways to learn from them, Park Day School and other progressive schools throughout America can join what is fast becoming an unusually healthy and productive national trend. Theatrical improvisers have long sworn by the motto that "mistakes are gifts." More recently, some of our economy's most successful innovators, the technocrats of Silicon Valley, have also embraced this philosophy, captured in their slogan: "Fail early; fail fast; and fail often." As the former journalist Kathryn Schulz, who bills herself as the "world's leading wrongologist," explained in her TED Talk in 2011, "Most of us spend the better part of our lives avoiding being wrong," but that "far from being a sign of intellectual inferiority, the capacity to err is crucial to human cognition."

All this is why I take issue with so many folk today who boast that their schools are "geared for success." Honestly, I'm waiting for a school to bravely tout itself as "geared for failure." That would signal the influence of educators who understand that in our complex modern world, it is errors and failures that most often lead to discovery and genuine learning.

Progressive educators' belief in child-centered education certainly doesn't assume that children should never be frustrated or uncomfortable as they learn. They should, and so should their teachers. The wisest teachers will do their best to build cultures that tolerate and even welcome that kind of temporary discomfort, together with ruthless honesty about the mistakes we make and how we can do better. This is how we maintain joy in learning and resilience. The teacher's job is to help guide students as they learn coping skills and how to persevere. Otherwise, we may all end up in a culture resembling a prefigured Lego design: shiny, perfect, and devoid of originality and surprise.

CHAPTER 8

The Petition
Promoting Social Justice

Park Day School students carry signs for Pride Day.
Photograph by John Orbon

The people in this room can make a difference in the world.

—Sign posted outside Susan Erb's first-grade classroom door

OPPRESSING THE "GREENIES"

Throughout America, year after year, fifth-graders study slavery as part of their required U.S. history curriculum. But how many of these ten- and eleven-year-olds are truly changed by the experience? How many are sufficiently emotionally engaged to remember what they've learned, much less find meaning in it? And how many manage to grow from the experience, gaining new compassion for those who are still oppressed today?

My efforts to answer these questions many years ago, when I was still a teacher and before I became head of school, helped lead to our well-remembered "Greenies" experiment, a plan I devised with my co-teacher, Aggie Brenneman.

Without any warning one morning, we assigned our fifth-grade students into two groups, based on the first letter of their last name. A–Ms were given coveted privileges, including extra time for recess, seats in front of the class, and first dibs on snacks and art supplies. Members of this group were also free to move around at will during class time. N–Zs were denied these perks, and required to sit still. They were also given green neckties to wear, to identify them as "Greenies."

Brenneman and I were surprised by how quickly and seriously the children took to the experiment. The privileged kids relished their new status and made no effort to share their special treats with any of the Greenies. Meanwhile, the Greenies brooded.

This lasted for two days. When students came to class on the third morning, Brenneman and I declared that we had made a mistake. We had really meant to privilege the kids in the Greenies group, we said. So now it was the other students' turn to wear the neckties.

Initially startled, the children soon settled into their new roles. And, once again, they surprised us. We'd imagined that the newly privileged students, who knew what it was like to be oppressed, would now have more empathy for the Greenies. Yet although a few indeed did, sneaking them treats from their stash, the majority instead were eager for revenge.

At one point, a boy who was newly part of the privileged group ripped up a paper, threw it on the floor, and ordered a Greenie to clean it up. Shortly thereafter, some of the Greenies tore off their neckties in protest. And later that same day, by telephone at home —this was well before the days of social media—the new Greenies organized a revolt. At a designated time the following morning, they were going to walk en masse out of class and rally in the schoolyard. Brenneman later learned that even her own first-grade daughter had joined the conspiracy to "overthrow the government."

We teachers were keeping in close touch with parents and soon caught wind of the plot. We squelched the rebellion before it got started, abandoned the simulation, and gathered the class to review what we had learned.

Yet again, I was surprised—this time by the emotional force of the students' reaction, and my own. We spent nearly two hours that day and another hour the next giving each child the opportunity to talk. There was anger, frustration, and bitterness. Some of the kids broke down in tears. In the end, every one of them expressed shock and shame at how they had treated the Greenies.

It hardly needs saying that the Greenies' sufferings in no way approached the cruelty experienced by slaves. Yet as the students embarked on their studies, they paid a qualitatively different kind of attention, engaged by their emotions and personal experience.

Not one parent complained about the experiment, and several cheered us on. Even so, Brenneman and I decided that the role play was too upsetting for children this young, and we never repeated our experiment. I might not have made this decision, however, had I known what I know now. As I worked on this book, Brenneman reached out by e-mail to several of the Greenies veterans, now in their early forties. Everyone she contacted vividly remembered the experiment, and several maintained that it had changed their lives for the better.

At present, Brenneman's daughter, Amy, owns a company that makes handbags and fashion accessories, and that donates a percentage of its profits to help victims of cluster bombs in Southeast Asia. Another Greenies veteran, Oregon high school teacher John Cornet, created and coordinates his school's Student-Mediation Dispute Resolution program, and was a recent finalist for the state's Teacher of the Year. Still another, Tierra Forte, works for a Fair Trade organic clothing company, and is married to another ex-Greenie, Jesse Simons, who is chief of staff of the Sierra Club. "I can't say if that one experience pushed me into what I'm doing today, but I would say it was Exhibit A of the way Park Day School tried to teach us to be really aware people," Simons said. "These things leave an imprint at such an early age, and having a small taste of what it would be like to be systematically oppressed—that stuck with me."

Even class members who aren't in explicitly do-good professions said the Greenies experience influenced them well into adulthood. Jenny Raven, a prominent East Bay pastry chef, called the exercise "one of the most resonant guiding lessons of my life." While she's not actively involved in social causes, she says, "I feel it's my responsibility to speak up whenever I see injustice, if someone is treated unfairly."

BEYOND COMMUNITY SERVICE

In many ways, the progressive tradition of encouraging social agency and awareness in students has never been more important than it is today. Despite unprecedented new challenges to young people's futures—from a dramatically changing job market to the growing risk of climate change—political apathy is rising among youth who by various reports are overwhelmed by the magnitude of these problems and skeptical that our current political leaders are seriously trying to address them. The United States now has the lowest voter turnout in the world among advanced democracies, particularly when it comes to our young. Barely 41 percent of voters aged eighteen to twenty-four turned out in the hotly contested 2012 presidential election.

Young people today are significantly less likely than in generations past to volunteer for campaigns or run for office. A leading electoral expert, Curtis Gans, has chalked this up in part to a decline in the quality of education in America's cities, a view strengthened by surveys showing a disturbing general lack of awareness and understanding of major events in the daily news. For example, a *National Geographic* poll found that even three years into the U.S. war with Iraq, six in ten young American adults couldn't locate that country on a map.

The trouble unfortunately goes deeper. An article in the *New York Times* in March 2014 ticked off the disturbing findings of a Pew Research Center survey, which found that the Millennial generation, those between eighteen and thirty-three, was drifting away from traditional institutions such as political parties and even marriage. Half of this age group described themselves as political independents and 29 percent said they didn't affiliate with any religion. Barely 26 percent were married, compared to 48 percent of baby boomers when they were the same age, and 65 percent of the members of the silent generation. Saddest of all, in my opinion, only 19 percent of Millennials said they felt most people could be trusted, compared with 40 percent of baby boomers.

Many people in my generation rightly fret over the sense of entitlement we witness in children. Studies have found that young people are becoming less empathetic and more interested in getting rich. The therapist and author Madeline Levine told our conference in Los Angeles of one eight-year-old boy she had met who told her he aspired to be a venture capitalist—and a girl of the same age who said her dream was to *marry* a venture capitalist. Madeline described her distress as she has realized that "the conversation I used to hear all the time in my office about helping the world . . . that has ended."

I fear most conventional schools and even, alas, some nominally progressive schools bear responsibility for this sad state of affairs. When it comes to public service, most students shy away from anything more than the perfunctory few hours that high-schoolers log in, serving meals to the homeless or cleaning stray animals' cages, to fulfill a hollow school requirement or pad a college application. Meanwhile, a major disincentive for students to engage with the world of social activism is most schools' deep aversion to discussing politics in the classroom, in part for fear of alienating parents in our polarized era.

In contrast, I'm convinced teachers can and should cultivate children's sense of obligation to a larger community and give them the basic tools to contribute to our democracy. That means teaching them the skills of rational argument, protest, and the use of petitions, much as a carpenter might tutor his or her apprentice in the use of the table saw and drill press. It also means inspiring them to care. On a visit to his alma mater, the Punahou School in Hawaii, after being elected to the U.S. Senate, President Obama reminisced about an ethics class he had taken, saying the school obliged students to reflect on questions including: "What does it mean to live in a diverse society? What does it mean to treat people with respect and dignity? What do we owe other people who are less fortunate than ourselves? What kinds of claims can we make in terms of creating the kind of society that benefits everybody, not just some people?"

At Park Day, one of our most important priorities is that our students feel a sense of agency, that they can make a difference in the world and have a duty to try. Together with other teachers who share that commitment at progressive schools throughout the nation, we guide children through a lot of early practice in the skills of awareness, compassion, and altruism. This can include not only "Greenies"-type simulations but far more ambitious philanthropic programs. One of my favorites of these is an annual event at the Casco Bay High School, a progressive public school in Portland, Maine, which sends its junior class to places such as New Orleans or a coal-mining community in West Virginia to work on community service projects and produce original video documentaries on Americans living in poverty. The Casco Bay students raise funds that pay all the costs of their trips, proving that kids don't need to go to a high-tuition private school to engage in a degree of social action rare in today's conventional schools. In another example, elementary school students at the Odyssey Charter School in Pasadena, another explicitly progressive public school, hold annual charity marketplaces, where they sell items created by student-run businesses, which make things like scarves, keychains, and stuffed animals, and divide what annually amounts to several thousand dollars in proceeds between their school and four local non-profits that they've previously studied in depth.

Research shows such practice can make a big difference in children's futures. One 2013 study suggests that Buddhist meditation teachers have been right all along: compassion can be trained over time, resulting in increased altruism. Researchers have also repeatedly found that people of all ages are more motivated to learn when they can see the usefulness of what they're learning and also use the information to do something that has a positive impact on others in their community.

With these considerations in mind, I was always disappointed at Park Day whenever too much time went by without students petitioning me over some perceived unfairness or plan to improve the school—or the world. Happily, this was rare.

Because students knew I was open to hearing them, they never hesitated to knock on my door. In a minor but memorable example a few years ago, a group of second-graders brought me a signed petition to reduce the number of swings a given student could take on our playground swing set before yielding to another child. I encouraged them to collaborate to solve that problem. They were the schoolyard swing experts, after all. And so they did, coming up with a new protocol for swing turns that has lasted to this day.

I didn't always approve such requests. When middle-schoolers lobbied to lift our ban on tree-climbing, I had to explain that our old, weak-limbed trees weren't up for that challenge, nor was our school insurance firm. Still, I believe the children went away feeling heard, if not triumphant.

Beyond our playground policies, Park Day School has worked to be a beacon of political awareness and engagement, both in what we stand for as a school and the way we teach our children. We consider ourselves a private school with a major public mission.

We don't court controversy, nor do we avoid it. That's a big part of our progressive tradition.

THE ROOTS OF RELEVANCE

The sharp increase in urban misery that accompanied America's Industrial Revolution inspired unprecedented popular concern and activism. In 1887, the Danish-American journalist Jacob Riis took advantage of the new invention of flash powder for photography to explore the dark streets and dim interiors of tenement homes, documenting the lives of New York's deprived underclass in his landmark book, *How the Other Half Lives*. Theodore Roosevelt called the book "an enlightenment and an inspiration," and he wasn't alone. Two years later, Jane Addams, the social worker and future Nobel Prize winner, helped establish one of the first of America's "settlement houses" on the West Side of Chicago. The idea, which had originated in England, was that privileged citizens and students should settle in poor urban neighborhoods to help improve residents' lives, research the causes of their poverty, and lobby for reform. The settlements provided health services, job counseling, English lessons for new immigrants, and even some education programs for immigrant children.

Through this route, Addams became one of the founding matriarchs of the Progressive Education movement. Her center of operations was known as Hull House, named after its builder, Charles Hull, and by 1900 it had grown to include a gymnasium, pool, book bindery, rooms for working women, and a meeting place for labor organizations. Addams publicized the efforts in her prolific writings and public speeches, and with her colleagues, a half-dozen other university-educated women, successfully lobbied for reforms that included the nation's first juvenile court. A fierce opponent of American involvement in World War I, she founded the Women's International League for Peace and Freedom in 1919, and worked for many years to get the great powers to disarm, winning the Nobel Peace Prize in 1931.

Addams was one of the earliest and strongest proponents of the theory that schools should awaken children's social conscience, complaining that teachers who limited a child's study to books failed to give that student "any clew [sic] to the life about him, or any power to usefully or intelligently connect himself with it." Among other goals, Addams wanted young people who were destined for factory jobs to study and better understand the history and dynamics of industry and labor, so that they could become more than cogs in the machine. Her idea was that these youth would imbue their work with a sense of social conscience that would make their lives more meaningful, while also helping create better working conditions. "It takes thirty-nine people to make a coat in a modern tailoring establishment, yet those same thirty-nine people might produce a coat in a spirit of 'team work' which would make the entire process as much more exhilarating than the work of the old solitary tailor, as playing in a baseball nine gives more pleasure to a boy than afforded by a solitary game of hand ball on the side of the barn."

Around the same time as Addams was setting up Hull House in Chicago, Felix Adler, the German-born son of a rabbi, founded his Society for Ethical Culture in New York City. Adler, then just twenty-four years old, campaigned against child labor and worked to improve conditions for residents of the city's overcrowded, disease-ridden tenement buildings. He joined with others to create a company that built model, affordable apartments on Manhattan's Lower East Side; and in 1878 he established a free kindergarten called the Workingman's School, which several years later became the Ethical Culture School that still exists today. Adler seemed to echo Addams's sentiments in 1902 when he said, "The ideal of the school is not the adaptation of the individual to the existing social environment; it is to develop individuals who are competent to change their environment in greater conformity with moral ideals."

John Dewey, the movement's standard-bearer, also championed a strong role for schools in awakening students' social consciousness and activism. Dewey made no secret of his own strong political opinions. Along with many other progressive reformers, he believed that industrialization had awarded great wealth to a small group of people, rather than benefiting all of society, while he dismissed the two major political parties as "the errand boys of big business." He served as president of the People's Lobby, a populist group, and tried to help create a third political party for the 1948 elections.

This politically charged, "social reconstructionist" faction of Progressive Education has endured through the decades—as was demonstrated by the presence of William Ayers and Angela Davis at our 2013 convention. Still, as I've mentioned, it has never been a universally shared position, even in Dewey's heyday, and Cold War witch-hunts of the 1950s deepened the division between those of us who wanted schools to help reshape society and those who yearned to leave politics outside the classroom doors. The schism endures today, and maybe even has widened with the further polarization of American politics. I understand the reasons behind this, yet have been repeatedly frustrated to see how hesitant so many progressive heads of school have become about prioritizing political agency—the training in those carpenter's tools of democracy.

Although some institutions remain brave exceptions to this rule, too many are content to limit their political engagement to the safest possible activities, such as having kids watch a video about Cesar Chavez or memorize Martin Luther King, Jr.'s, "I Have a Dream" speech. I suppose it shouldn't have surprised me, and yet I expected that more of the school leaders I interviewed would have emphasized, or at least mentioned, their social justice goals when defining Progressive Education. I chalked up their reticence to our society's broader drift away from community engagement and activism, yet continue to feel there's a much stronger role for schools to play here, both in our own behavior and in the lessons we impart to our students.

WALKING OUR TALK

As adults—teachers and parents—we know that our students and children are constantly observing us, scanning us for signs of hypocrisy or incongruence between our statements and actions. That's a hefty responsibility, particularly given some of our schools' strong language about social action in their mission statements. The Cambridge Friends School, for instance, says: "We expect all students to develop their intellectual, physical, creative, and spiritual potential and, through the example of their lives, to challenge oppression and to contribute to justice and understanding in the world." The mission statement on the Web site of the Ethical Culture Fieldston School in New York says it aims to create "passionate learners, critical thinkers, and ethical individuals who aim to make the world more humane and just."

Happily, in many cases our schools have served as worthy models of these aspirations. Even before the civil rights era, several progressive schools were among the first to enroll African-American students. Presidio Hill School, integrated in the 1940s, was the first independent school in San Francisco to do so, while Georgetown Day School, founded in 1945, became the first integrated school in Washington, D.C. In Alexandria, Virginia, the Burgundy Farm Country Day School, founded in 1946 by a group of idealistic parents including the celebrated television journalist Eric Sevareid, began actively seeking African-American students as early as 1950. And today, as I've described, many of our schools are standard-bearers for other diversity issues, standing up for the rights of gay, lesbian, and transgender students.

In several cases, our schools' choices of location speak volumes. At Park Day School, we decided in our first years to establish ourselves in Oakland, rather than wealthier Berkeley, and in Oakland's "flats," rather than the comparatively privileged hills, making it easier to attract and retain working-class families. Similarly, the Children's Community School in Van Nuys, California, founded in 1972, is set in a neighborhood of mostly inexpensive, multi-unit dwellings. Among progressive public schools, Mission Hill School in Boston was established in 1997 in the historic but then high-crime Jamaica Plain neighborhood. And the Namaste K–8 Charter School, which doesn't formally call itself progressive but follows many of our core principles, established itself in 2004 on the depressed southwest side of Chicago, enrolling children mostly from low-income Latino and African-American families.

In many other cases, our choice of location reflects our strong environmental values. Several of our schools, such as the Putney School in Vermont and the Burgundy Farm Country Day School in Virginia, are set on conserved farmland, where students spend a good deal of time outdoors, caring for animals and studying nature. In 1967, the Burgundy Farm School acquired the 500-acre Burgundy Center for Wildlife Studies, where students now partake in twice-a-year immersion programs. The Manhattan Country School, founded in 1966, has two locations, on the Upper West Side and on a farm in Roxbury, New York. Meanwhile, the Crossroads School for Arts and Sciences in Santa Monica, California, created three full-time positions for its environmental program, which includes overnight trips for field study and community service; while the Capitol Hill Day School in Washington, D.C., orchestrates some twenty field trips a year to get students out in nature.

Decisions about tuition are another fundamental way that private progressive schools walk our talk. Alas, so many of our schools, despite their noble language, are located in wealthy suburbs and charge such high tuitions that at our 2009 conference in Washington, D.C., Francisco Guajardo, an associate professor of educational leadership at the University of Texas–Pan American, challenged us to work harder to make our student bodies more reflective of American racial and economic diversity.

Even so, together with Park Day School, many progressive schools take justified pride in aggressive financial aid programs that maintain economic and racial diversity that goes well beyond window-dressing. At the Children's Community School in Van Nuys, Neal Wrightson notes that more than 40 percent of students receive financial aid, requiring a commitment of up to a quarter of annual tuition revenue. For less privileged students, the school covers costs of hot lunches and field trips, including the trip to study island culture in Hawaii, which I described earlier. "Our policy is that every student goes on every trip, so we cover whatever portion (including all) of the cost they cannot manage," Wrightson told me.

My favorite example of a school that is truly progressive in the way it handles tuition is that of the Manhattan Country School, where the maximum tuition is $39,900 for fifth through eighth grades, yet where student enrollment is abundantly diverse in terms both of race and economic status. Rather than award scholarships or financial assistance, as so many of our schools take pride in doing, the Manhattan Country School goes further, by using a sliding scale. The school requires all families, rich and poor alike, to submit a confidential financial worksheet every year, after which a fee is set for each family, according to its ability to pay. To Jennifer Morgan-Bennett, a college professor and the mother of a child of color, the sliding scale represents the "radical" rejection of the notion "that wealthy people simply are accepted into a school on their child's intellectual merit, while the poorer child has to win an 'award.' It means that the cost of educating our children is borne by all of us according to our abilities, and that those of us who either start as or end up as full paying families have no more 'natural' access to the benefits of education than anyone else. It means that our school is a community comprised of a range of families united by the commitment to educate any child, not just my child." For her daughter Emma, more specifically, it meant a childhood of attending sleepovers in multimillion-dollar con- dos and tiny apartments, riding on subways and in luxury cars, and understanding that people can bridge great differences for the sake of friendship and community.

The school encourages such experiences by, among other things, requiring every new five-year-old to host a class visit for lunch at his or her home—a simple but profound experience that exposes children to a wide variety of cultural and eco- nomic circumstances. When questions about differences arise, the teachers openly confront them, allowing students a safe place to grapple with stereotypes and harsh realities. This is the way the director of Manhattan Country School, Michèle Solá, puts into practice her belief, as she related on my visit to her school, that Progressive Education is "education serving the possibilities democracy sets forth. It acknowledges that soci- ety is not yet perfect and in achieving those possibilities and recognizing the places where there are incongruities, educa- tion can be a productive base where people can be hopeful about making change."

Although we haven't reached the point of establishing a sliding scale at Park Day, I'm proud of both the way we've pursued and achieved diversity in our student body and our determined and groundbreaking partnerships with public schools, one of the strongest such programs in the nation.

Our Oakland location puts us right next door to the Oakland Technical High School and down the street from Emerson Elementary School, both public schools with high levels of enrollment of children from low-income families. We have ongoing programs with these schools and others to share some of the privileges we don't want our students to take for granted. One example is our annual book drive, when we collect up to 3,000 children's books to donate to a local public school. In the process, many Park Day students confront the reality that they have more books in their homes than some of our nearby schools have in their libraries.

The touchy issue on this front and others, and a constant source of discussion for us, is how to avoid a *noblesse oblige* factor—making children from privileged families feel entitled while making others feel awkward and indebted. Deborah Meier and other progressive leaders raise the very good point that until we achieve some fundamental structural changes in our country, tuition grants and partnerships can have only relatively minimal impacts. As Meier has written, even the relatively poor U.S. test scores on international reading and math tests reflect less the problems with America's educational system than with our increasingly skewed income distribution. All you have to do is remove the kids living in poverty from each nation's score, and America comes in near the top. We simply have more students living in poverty than nations scoring higher than us. "We don't have a crisis in education," Meier told our conference in Los Angeles. "We have a crisis in democracy."

From my perspective, that's all the more reason that we as educators must make sure new generations have the tools they need for social change.

CLASS-CONSCIOUSNESS

A constant theme for students at most progressive schools is that they can make a difference in the world—and that they have an obligation to do so. "Everything we do has a social purpose," says my colleague Adriana Murphy, at the Friends Community School in College Park, Maryland. "When we teach kids to write, for instance, the purpose isn't just to fill out a worksheet, it's to interact in society, to be able to communicate your ideas and other people's ideas and to use that education to make the world better." In this way, she says, students get the message that they're expected to contribute—not just after they graduate, but in the here and now.

At the schools that take this idea seriously, "community service" is no item to be checked off a list. Murphy's seventh-graders must thoroughly study the options among local non-profits before choosing a cause to which to devote their community service time. In eighth grade, the students move on to learning how to advocate for the cause in which they believe. Working with a mentor based outside the school, in an organization that campaigns for their chosen pursuit, they may engage in activities such as writing letters to a member of Congress or a newspaper editor and attending protest demonstrations. "To me, democracy is at its best the more time its citizens have to appreciate its value," says Murphy, adding, "Age twelve or thirteen isn't a bad place to start!"

Most progressive educators consider it part of their job to guide students to respond intelligently to current events. And in many schools, students are taking the lead. Within days after the fatal shooting of twenty children and six adult staff members at the Sandy Hook Elementary School in Newtown, Connecticut, high school students at the Ethical Culture Fieldston School formed a committee against gun violence. Over the next year, about thirty students met regularly (usually weekly), together with half a dozen faculty members, while also joining protest rallies at City Hall in support of new gun laws, and calling and e-mailing state representatives. In December 2013, the group hosted a campus Day to End Gun Violence, with workshops led by students, outside speakers, and faculty members.

This wasn't an isolated example. The Ethical Culture students have formed groups to raise aid money for Haiti and Senegal, and to build awareness and action on fracking, fossil-fuel divestment, and gender and transgender issues. "It's not that teachers are urging kids to do this," says the dean of students, Nancy Banks. "It's part of the mission of the school, to train people to go out and change the world. The students know that this is a school where it's possible to do that, and the community values activism and a commitment to social justice. So often the teacher's job is just to get out of the students' way."

Direct experience engages children's emotions, increasing motivation. Thus, on Martin Luther King Day, students at the Manhattan Country School join with parents and teachers to march for civil rights through the streets of New York City. I wasn't surprised to learn that two school alumni have since started their own charter schools to serve disadvantaged students in New York.

At Park Day, as with everything we teach, we take care to engage students in social justice projects in ways that suit their evolving understanding. Thus, after our teachers encourage kindergartners and first-graders to start thinking of other children's feelings, they'll coax them to broaden their perspectives.

In second and third grade, students investigate their family histories, relating their stories in terms of issues of cultural differences, immigration, and civil rights. In fourth and fifth grades, they learn about media awareness, stereotypes, and how to consider issues from different perspectives. In middle school, the kids study the impact of prejudice and intolerance, with activities that include a voluntary day of silence, in order to understand what it's like to not be heard.

Throughout all this time, the children aren't just studying: they're actively participating, whether it's by picking up trash around the campus at lunch hour, tutoring younger kids in math and reading, sorting or labeling books for our book drive, or acting in our annual sixth-grade plays.

These plays are major productions, and for the past several years, they have been politically charged. For many years, they were written by just three of us—Aggie Brenneman of the "Greenies" experiment, Harriet Cohen, and me—with topics ranging from the U.S. labor movement to civil rights struggles to the 1929 stock market crash to the McCarthy era to Watergate. One play began with a conversation between Mahatma Gandhi, Nelson Mandela, and Martin Luther King, Jr., discussing groups of people who have had their rights denied.

One of our most memorable projects was *A Journey to Understanding: Echoes of Afghanistan*, produced in 2002, in the wake of the 9/11 attacks. Our faculty shared the feeling that this unprecedented disaster, and the two wars that followed, required an especially thoughtful response. Most of our students, together with students throughout the nation, had no idea who these strange-seeming people who had attacked us were, or why they had done such a thing, or what we hoped to accomplish by invading their country. The play would be an opportunity to learn about all these issues, to confront their fear and sadness and emerge with something more hopeful.

In the days after the event, Brenneman asked her sixth-graders to write down what they were feeling. Their responses became the opening lyrics of the play, with the melodies composed by our music whiz, Harriet Cohen. The story proceeded with the students wanting to know more, and finally traveling to Afghanistan. At the play's end, the children conclude that people in Afghanistan:

> . . . want food and shelter
> For their families . . .
> Healthy, peaceful lives for their children . . .
> To pursue their dreams through education . . .
> And to live their lives without oppression . . .
> Isn't it the same for me and you?
> . . . With all that divides us,
> There's more that can bind us
> Throughout this global community
> And knowledge will give us
> The wisdom and power
> To work for what the world should be.

Zoe Mercer-Golden, who is Jewish and was then in the sixth grade, vividly remembers the two months she and her friends spent wearing Afghan costumes and performing Afghan songs and dances. Yet what influenced her even more strongly that year was hearing at school about how Middle Easterners throughout America had become victims of hate crimes in the wake of 9/11. After a friend with Sikh relatives told her that turban-wearing Sikhs were being attacked on the street, Zoe recalled, "I, and others in our friend group, were aghast. Who could be so full of hate that they would attack innocent people?" Two months after the 9/11 attacks, the friends organized a "Walk of Acceptance" to raise money for the victims of hate crimes. They made fliers and posters during their lunch breaks and, with their teachers' support, visited other classrooms to invite students and parents to participate. Cathy Shields, the school's event and volunteer coordinator, called local newspaper reporters. More than two hundred people, mostly from Park Day, joined the walk, and Zoe and a friend gave their first speeches as activists on the shores of Lake Merritt. They raised $3,000 for their cause, which they donated to a hotline run by a local Arab and Muslim organization.

"I didn't learn until I changed schools the following year exactly how unusual this series of experiences was," Zoe has told me. "None of my classmates at my new college-prep school knew anything substantial about Afghanistan. None had learned about hate crimes; none had been given the chance to organize a community event or perform in public to educate others."

As America went to war—first in Iraq and then in Afghanistan—Park Day's focus on the Middle East continued, and so did Zoe's activism. At age eleven, along with her friend Valerie Bisharat, a ten-year-old Palestinian student, Zoe proposed the idea for an annual magazine that would be produced together with children living in the Palestinian city of Ramallah on the West Bank. The project, called *Children Without Borders*, continues to this day, featuring interviews between the students (conducted on Skype), and focused on local traditions, holidays, hobbies, recipes, sports, and other non-political interests. As the de facto publisher of this enterprise, I forbade any mention of topics relating to politics, soldiers, terrorism, or checkpoints—a ban that led to quite a few conflicts over alleged censorship with the students and even their adult editors, two Park Day faculty members. But I doubt the magazine would have survived this long or this well if it had strayed into that sort of hullabaloo. As it is, the project has won national acclaim, including being honored at the 2004 conference of the Peace and Justice Studies Association.

As I've said, we don't court controversy, but nor do we shy away from it. Which I suppose is just one reason that on a breezy March afternoon in 2003 I found myself in the unusual position, for a head of school, of leading thirty-one sixth-graders down Broadway Avenue in Oakland, waving placards with slogans against that year's U.S. invasion of Iraq.

When the students first came to me with their request, I worried what parents might think. I also worried about whether they were old enough to withstand what would surely be some unfriendly reactions on the street. What I didn't worry about was where my own feelings about the war fit in. This was a question of the children's political agency, something we had been encouraging them to develop for years. I polled the parents by phone. Not one of them objected.

It was a different story that afternoon, however. Although some drivers honked in support, others shouted that we were un-American and disloyal. We didn't answer back, and on debriefing the sixth-graders afterwards at school, I was happy to hear that they had felt more empowered than belittled.

Now, was the march a case of actually courting the kind of controversy I've worked to keep at bay on our *Children Without Borders* magazine? It's a reasonable question. But from my perspective, the march was limited and local, and my presence with the children meant I could end it at any time. Letting politics into the magazine, which was born and has been maintained as a kid-to-kid venture with the goal of putting a face on children in the Middle East, would have differed by potentially exposing our students and our school to more serious and lasting repercussions. The balance of costs and benefits simply wasn't the same.

For the most part, throughout my tenure at Park Day, I've been delighted to find that any time I've feared our strong policy of social engagement might be going too far, our extraordinary group of children and parents has proven me wrong. Rather than shrink back, they have contributed to pushing us on. In 2012, for example, our board extended our formal commitment to social justice, enacting a rule that four of the twenty-five hours of volunteer time required from every family be committed to helping the school advance its social justice agenda.

While it's common for private schools to require "volunteer" hours, our specification is unusual, if not unique. Yet we've been confident we're on the right track, as evidence accumulates that Park Day graduates have indeed been inspired by their time here to go out and make a difference in the world.

Take Zoe, whose outrage over unfairness to Sikhs as a sixth-grader led to her planning the Walk of Acceptance, and co-founding our *Children Without Borders* magazine. After earning degrees from Yale in English and art history, she took a job focused on improving access for people with disabilities at the Metropolitan Museum of Art. In 2014, she was bound for Brazil to teach English on a Fulbright scholarship. "Looking at my life today, I am struck by how much of what I did in college and what I'm doing now can be traced to Park Day," she wrote me. "Park Day has left a permanent legacy in my life of self-reflection and critical engagement with mainstream narratives, a bent towards conflict resolution and mediation, and a desire to serve and advocate for overlooked and undervalued communities. My classmates—many of them still my good friends—are the same. Each of us has chosen our own paths of activism and informed citizenship, but as a cohort and as individuals, we have stayed true to what we learned as sixth-graders."

Back to the Future

Tom Little celebrates Park Day School's thirtieth anniversary in the parking lot of the Masonic Hall in Oakland, in 2006.   Photograph by Ralph Granich Photography

We've been leaders of "21st-century education" for about 100 years.

—SCOTT MORAN, head of school at the progressive
K–6 Westland School in Los Angeles

"THE GOAL IS TO MAKE IT BIGGER"

On a sunny morning in January 2014, nineteen progressive educators from schools all over America, and two more who have come all the way

from Seoul, South Korea, have gathered in Park Day School's airy Great Room for the first meeting of the Progressive Education Network Institute. This meeting is a milestone for our movement, yet another sign of the reviving strength of our organization. For the next three days, the travelers will exchange ideas and worries, share meals and small talk, and muster their resolve to strengthen progressive teaching in their schools and throughout the nation.

I wish I could be there. Instead, I'm waiting for progress reports as I lay in a rented hospital bed, upstairs in my home just a few miles away. Within easy reach is my laptop, cellphone, notebook, walker, wheelchair, and my ever present, well-thumbed copy of Lawrence Cremin's history of Progressive Education. The institute co-leaders, my friends and colleagues Maureen Cheever and Dan Schwartz (head of school at the Baker Demonstration School in Wilmette, Illinois), have promised to call with updates, and I want to be ready to help if I can. It's an unseasonably warm morning, so my window is open, and I can hear children playing at recess in the schoolyard next door. The clamor is especially welcome today; after all, it's been the weekday soundtrack of my last nearly four decades.

As I'll learn later today, the institute students include several teachers, one principal, three administrators, and a graduate student, hailing from a mix of public and private schools. Some have arrived dressed in jeans and sweaters; others wear suits and dresses. Just now, they're taking a tour of our campus, led by Park Day School's interim head of school Jonathan Kidder. They're oohing and ahhing over our vegetable garden—the sugar snap peas, broccoli, and spinach all especially lush—and smiling at the photographs and children's artwork adorning our hallways. Kidder walks them by Joan Wright-Albertini's room and tells them the stories of her amazing ecosystem projects. I know what they're thinking: the school seems like a paradise. That's how I see it too, and have seen it every day for the past thirty-eight years.

Back in the Great Room, where full-length windows look out on pine trees and palms, the students settle down to business, arranging laptops near cups of coffee and glasses of orange juice. From what I learned on my trip to schools last spring, I could have predicted what they're saying.

"I don't know how to talk about Progressive Education, even though we do it every day," confesses Samantha Inglis, an elementary school teacher at the independent Chadwick School in Palos Verdes, in Southern California.

In contrast, Chris Collaros, head of the Wickliffe Elementary School, is more intent on learning how to cope with the institutional threats to progressive public schools like his own. Collaros had been feeling tremendous pressure from state and local authorities to teach in more standardized, "drill-and-kill" ways. "In Ohio, we're under assault," he says. "With high-stakes testing and teacher evaluation, it's spiraling out of control. I know in my gut why it's not good, but I want a way to articulate it."

Jay Dillon, a teacher of first and second grade from the public Winnetka School District outside Chicago, is feeling similar pressure. "My goal is to immerse myself with other people living this and understand how far I can move in the world in which I teach without pushing the cart over," he says. "I'm trying not to think of it as a partisan issue, but it feels like one."

Kate Miller, a fourth-grade teacher at the Children's School, the K–5 elementary school in the Chicago suburbs, adds an optimistic note: "We know that what we're doing works, and we have the responsibility to share our practices with other teachers. The goal is to make it bigger."

Cheever calls shortly after noon, as promised. "I can't wait to fill you in on the details," she tells me. "It was better than we even imagined." When she comes by the house two days later, she brings a poster board–sized orange card, the kind that classmates send home to a friend absent from school because of illness. "You were sorely missed," it says, "but clearly present in all we did." It even has a drawing on the front: of smiling students and a teacher.

RESTORING PRIDE IN THE "P-WORD"

At their first meeting in Washington, D.C., in 1919, the founding members of the Progressive Education Association declared their intent to have their schools be laboratories of new ideas and for them to become leaders of American schools.

Their wish came true for a few decades. But everything changed by the 1950s. The harsh backlash of those years against progressivism in all its incarnations not only reduced our numbers but added to the isolation of the schools that remained. Even on the west and east coasts, where progressive schools have been relatively numerous, we've only rarely collaborated, be it for professional development or anything else.

I'm happy to tell you, however, that in recent years the walls of these silos have started to fall.

Educators all over this country today are hungry for change, and specifically for models of teaching and learning that make more sense for stressed kids in our globalized economy. The burden of high-stakes tests and the clumsy initial rollout of the Common Core, on top of continuing signs that our system has been failing students and their families, are pushing many to seek alternatives. We recognize the problem is deeper than our education system. At our 2013 convention in Los Angeles, the therapist Madeline Levine captured the problem when she spoke of an "incredible misalignment between cultural notions of what success and education look like and what's really in the best interests of kids both in terms of healthy child development and engagement with learning."

At the extreme end of this national frustration is radical resistance—from students, parents, and "badass" teachers, as I've already described. Still, saying no isn't our only response. Progressive and other concerned educators have also been devising creative alternatives, often based on our legacy from Dewey, Parker, Pratt, and so many others before us. Those of us who believe that the Common Core represents at least potential progress—and I count myself among the many who do—are concerned that it will fail, just like so many other grand ideas before it, if we simply attempt to impose new content and standards without adding some fundamentally different classroom strategies. It probably won't surprise you to hear of my conviction that the answer lies in reviving and ramping up the basic progressive strategies I've described to you in these pages, including placing more emphasis on eliciting and engaging students' interests, combined with project-based learning, integrated curriculum, strong school communities, and real-world relevance.

With that in mind, I've been excited to watch the increasing success of a number of recent bold attempts to transform schools with strategies in the very best of our progressive traditions. I'll describe two exemplary programs that are, happily, focused on America's deserving public schools.

The first is a network known as Big Picture Learning, established in 1995 by two out-of-the-box educators, Dennis Littky and Elliot Washor, who have challenged the prevailing, passive, cookie-cutter model with schools in which teachers serve as guides to elicit student interest, and which de-emphasize grades and standardized tests while motivating kids to work with mentors, get real-world experience, and take responsibility for their own education. In a 2011 column for *Edutopia*, the two founders offered a striking example of this process, with the story of a student they called Sam.

Sam had arrived at one of the Big Picture schools after failing eighth grade. Yet by the time he reached his senior year, he was determined to pursue his keen interest in Wall Street's influence on Congress. In particular, he wanted to find out if there were any connections between financial firms' political contributions and their access to government bailout funds. With encouragement and support from his teachers, and using publicly available data, this student, who had previously had little use for algorithms as they were taught by his math teachers, developed original software that helped him pursue his theory and display the connections. It was an exceedingly sophisticated project for a high school student; yet Sam, with the right support, had discovered and been able to follow a passion keen enough to drive him.

The first Big Picture Learning project was the Metropolitan Regional Career and Technical Center. The school, known as "the Met," and based in Providence, Rhode Island, had an unusually large enrollment of "at-risk" African-American and Latino students. Yet the initial freshman class in 2000 had a 96 percent graduation rate, winning $500,000 total in college scholarship funds, a record matched or bettered by each subsequent graduating class. Those achievements won notice and funding from the Bill and Melinda Gates Foundation, which has helped Big Picture Learning rapidly expand its schools. Today, it boasts forty-four schools in the United States, twenty-five in Australia, and twenty-seven in Israel.

An equally impressive reform-minded network is Expeditionary Learning, launched in 1993, which at last count was collaborating with 160 schools in 33 states. The schools are based on the philosophy of Kurt Hahn, a progressive German-Jewish schoolmaster who courageously spoke out against the Nazis in the 1930s. Hahn is credited with inspiring the creation of Outward Bound, founded in 1941 to train young sailors in survival skills, and which later developed into an exceptionally successful program to help troubled youth gain self-esteem through physical challenges. Expeditionary Learning became a chartered entity of Outward Bound, emphasizing project-based learning expeditions, in which students engage in interdisciplinary, in-depth study of compelling topics, with assessments based on public presentations and portfolios. (In the previous chapter, I mentioned one of those projects, at the Casco Bay High School in Maine, in which students produce video documentaries of impoverished Americans.) The Expeditionary Learning Network—in an all-too-rare practice, and to its great credit—keeps track of its student achievement, and has found that schools using its model consistently outperform district averages on state and mandated tests, often by substantial margins and with particular success among African-American and Latino students.

Of course, it will take much more than a few new school networks, however brilliant their success, to turn around the great battleship of the U.S. education system. That's why I'm rooting for the Progressive Education Network to be a stronger leader in the coming months and years, long after I won't be here to cheer its members on.

Our national conventions have been growing dramatically, and our PEN Institute is another big step forward. Its new training effort adds to several other promising attempts to popularize progressive approaches. In San Diego, the widely acclaimed High Tech High public charter school network, founded in 2000 by local business leaders intent on elevating the quality of the local pool of potential employees, recently established its own on-site graduate school, with the stated aim of being recognized throughout the world as "a hub of progressive practice related to teaching and learning, and as a model of thoughtful, integrated, and transformative graduate education that has a direct impact on K–12 schools." On the east coast, there's the

Progressive Education Lab, established in 2009 as a two-year-long apprenticeship program for teachers, and run by four progressive schools based in Massachusetts, New York, and Vermont. Add to this the new Progressive Teaching Institute, inaugurated in 2012 and offered during summers at the Ethical Culture Fieldston School in New York City.

Over the past two decades, several advocacy organizations have sprung up to campaign for progressive reforms, among them the Coalition of Essential Schools, Educators for Social Responsibility, Teachers 4 Social Justice, the Forum for Education and Democracy, and the Center for Educational Renewal. PEN heartily supports their efforts, while my great hope is that in the near future, we can collaborate together to become ever stronger and more effective. Such collaboration should include not only dedicated advocacy groups but our natural—and powerful—allies in the numerous Montessori schools, many of which explicitly refer to themselves as "progressive." We have too much in common to remain as separate as we've been for all these years.

One collaborative goal that could serve us all well—and, most important, serve students—will be to muster some of the abundant evidence supporting progressive strategies. As I've noted, the last comprehensive evaluation of progressive schools took place in the 1940s, with the so-called Eight-Year Study, commissioned by the Progressive Education Association. In the more than seventy years since then, no other group has even come close to replicating this work, and the dearth of research haunts progressive educators who, as more than one of our institute students has said, know what they're doing works but can't say why.

The best that many schools have been able to offer is evidence of how their alumni do on SATs and college admissions—

an uncomfortable irony, since we're often the first to question these metrics as markers of lifelong success and happiness. That's why I'm so encouraged by the research being done by the Putney School, in Vermont, which for the past six years has been gathering longitudinal data on its graduates that go far beyond simple facts about college acceptances and GPAs to track indicators of long-term well-being. "We're measuring an enormous amount of stuff because we don't really know what we're going to find," says Emily Jones, the head of school.

> We're looking at cultural attitudes, learning styles, beliefs about health, spirituality, and exposure to different cultures, among other things. While they're in school, we also keep track of family income, the education of parents, how long they spend on computers, what grades they're getting, visits to the health department, whether they play musical instruments, and whether they have food allergies. The kids answer a questionnaire every year that asks about things like attachment style, self-esteem, resilience, and empathy. And all the adults on campus answer the same questions, since we believe we're all part of the same petri dish.

Jones says her school embarked on this project after visitors repeatedly challenged the staff to explain its success. Its alumni include many celebrated envelope-pushers, such as the journalists Christian Lehmann-Haupt and J. Anthony Lukas, the controversial photographer Sally Mann, the actors Wallace Shawn and Felicity Huffman, the Olympic skiing medalist Bill Koch, the LinkedIn co-founder Reid Hoffman, and the celebrated American Greenpeace ship captain Peter Willcox. (In September 2013, Willcox was arrested in Murmansk, Russia, for his involvement in a protest in which several international activists tried to scale an offshore oil platform belonging to a state-owned oil-and-gas

company.) "We don't produce any worker bees—or rather, whenever I come across one, I ask myself, 'What happened *here?*'" says
Jones. She says she expects she'll be able to come up with some
of the answers she's looking for around the time the first class of
students being studied turns thirty-four. I hope the Progressive
Education Network might sponsor its own in-depth research,
perhaps using the Putney School study as a model.

While we're waiting for new data, however, there's much that we
can do right now to establish our evidence-based bona fides. I
have tried, in these pages, to clearly articulate the main strategies involved in modern Progressive Education and to show that
in each case, there is abundant and often recent research available to support them.

For the future—and here I'll take a moment to directly
address my fellow heads of schools—we all need to keep plugged
in to the flood of neuroscience research that in many cases is
offering solid evidence for our practices. When parents feel anxious about their child's academic progress in a progressive school
that eschews mainstream standards, we educators need solid
data, not just anecdotes, to show how that child is being engaged
intellectually and developing cognitively and emotionally.

What's more, our audience can't just be parents. Progressive
educators must develop a stronger, unified voice to reach
regional and national policymakers.

Now, some have suggested that to do this most effectively, it's
time to modernize our brand and jettison the name "progressive," with all of its historical baggage. Several schools I visited
on my cross-country pilgrimage—even some with strong roots
in our century-old traditions—have already stopped explicitly
calling themselves progressive, disinfecting their Web sites and

promotional materials of any mention of the word, substituting adjectives like "innovative," without much apparent irony. "I don't bandy the word around as much as my predecessors," one school leader told me, adding that he and his staff were "deliberately repackaging what it means to be a progressive school, to really speak to the needs of the parents who are interested in twenty-first-century learning."

After all this time together, I suspect you can imagine my frustration in hearing this. In fact, I believe now is our time to be bold, and to reclaim our heritage with renewed pride. And indeed, I'm seeing lots of signs that the p-word is coming back in style. On New Year's Day 2014, when Bill de Blasio, whom MSNBC has hailed as an "unapologetic progressive," took office as mayor of America's most powerful city, the *New York Times* front page used the word "progressive" half a dozen times.

It looks more and more like this is our moment.

HISTORY REPEATED—AND A MOVEMENT REKINDLED

Two months have gone by since I waited for news of our first PEN Institute. It is late March 2014; the wisteria is blooming in our small front garden, a cheerful sight that unfortunately also reminds me of the precious passing time. It has already been seven months since the doctors told me I could expect another year or so at best.

The PEN Institute fellows plan to reunite in New York, at the Manhattan Country School, in late April, but once again, I won't be with them. After a few months of welcome reprieve, thanks to chemo, my cancer has abruptly begun to spread more rapidly. Now, walking even short distances is challenging. I spend my time reading, e-mailing, and conversing with my wife Elizabeth, a professional meditation coach who has wisely chosen this time to deepen her spiritual studies. There's also a constant stream of visitors—the teachers I've known for decades, former Park Day parents and students, and my two adult children, Courtney and Matt. The dining-room table is filled with bouquets—orchids, roses, and pungent lilies—and casseroles delivered by our thoughtful friends.

It's an extraordinarily awkward privilege, this business of having a year, more or less, to say goodbye. I'm both honored and embarrassed by the many public tributes I've had over these past seven months: at my retirement ceremony, in Park Day's Great Room, there was a moment when I struggled for composure, on the dais, looking out at a couple hundred upturned faces of such dear friends. "Who gets this?" I finally asked, and then, drawing on a dim recollection of Lou Gehrig's famous speech as illness forced him to leave his beloved Yankees, I said that I, too, felt like the luckiest man on the face of the earth. This truly is what I believe: I've had a loving marriage, terrific children, and thirty-eight years of working in a profession I would choose again in a heartbeat.

Now, as I alternate between my hopes for the future and this daily business of dying, I think about the repetitive cycles in our national history of creation and destruction and creation once again. In several striking and unfortunate ways, conditions in twenty-first-century America have come to resemble those of a century past. These include historic levels of income inequality; a widening concentration of riches and power in the hands of a few; and a breakdown in government effectiveness. Added to these are grave new threats, from nuclear proliferation to climate change, demanding urgent responses from government and society.

Then, as now, a "gilded age" of fabulous wealth and luxury contrasts with high unemployment, growing poverty, and building resentment. Then, as now, America's schools—historically our guardians of democracy and gateway to equal opportunity—are perceived to be failing.

Amid all this, our times are distinguished by an air of extraordinary change and opportunity that also has a great deal in common with the mood of the Progressive Era. Back then, the Second Industrial Revolution transformed lives with new inventions such as the household light bulb and the Model T. Today, a third and even more transformative industrial revolution has brought us the Internet, smartphones, and a broad range of new, renewable energy sources. Some of these technologies are already pushing our schools in potentially progressive directions, whether or not that's what they want. The Internet has liberated information, so that students can—and do—spend more time pursuing their own interests, from overindulging in video games to creating new activist groups or searching for more environmentally sustainable ways to live. Our newly computerized world has made communication much easier, faster, and informal, which has isolated and endangered some children, putting them at risk of losing real-world ties or being victimized by predators, while giving others new ways to choose and find communities that may stretch thousands of miles away from their home.

My big question is to what extent we'll evolve to surpass our problems and seize our opportunities. Again, it will depend on our leadership—and here I'm glad to say that after my visits to progressive schools, I'm quite hopeful that all will be well.

I'm thinking of three leaders in particular. The first would be Neal Wrightson, the veteran director of the Children's Community School in Van Nuys. I can see him clearly in my memory, standing tall on the dais at the Biltmore Hotel in Los Angeles last October, as he reminded us all of our responsibility for no less than the future of America's democracy. "This fight over what it means to be educated, and the purpose of schools, is a pitched battle in which both sides know what they are fighting for," he said. "Progressive Education was founded on the idea that schools have a fundamental responsibility to educate children to be activists, agents for change—to imagine a better world and then to work to make it so."

While Wrightson reminds us of our founding principles and glorious past, I also keep in mind my conversation with Adriana Murphy, the head of the middle school at the Friends Community School in College Park. Murphy, who belongs to a younger generation of teachers, told me that while older progressive educators may be more ideological—"flag-waving," as she said—the younger batch is just as committed to the practices and pedagogy, while perhaps also more prepared to defend them with new tools. She also has a keen sense of her responsibility to do that, from her perch at a school just fifteen miles from the national capital. "It is incumbent upon the second wave of progressive educators to take the research validating our principles that has been done in recent years, and put into practice what our foremothers and forefathers did not have at their disposal," she told me, "because what we've seen in education in the past twenty to thirty years just isn't working."

Murphy is particularly skillful in speaking to worried parents about the advantages of our model; she isn't shy, for instance, about dropping what she calls the "H-bomb": "There are kids who score at the top of their class and still get rejected from Harvard," she points out. "What top colleges are looking for is something more than striving for perfect grades. They want to see a work ethic, an ability to get along with others, and beyond that, this quality of being a linchpin—the indispensable person, who is connected, whom the organization can't live without. You take a look around and those tend to be the kids who graduate from progressive schools."

When I think of our movement's future, I also remember Ayla Gavins at Mission Hill. That small public school, with its wise financial stewardship and widely celebrated success rate with children representing a dramatically diverse mix of learning abilities, ethnic origins, and economic resources, perhaps best represents our hope of a renaissance. Fortunately, Gavins, together with Wrightson and Murphy, is one of those rare educators who can be eloquent about what she knows is working.

"I think this movement will grow, and there will be many more progressive schools," she says. "Teachers and parents are desperate for things to be different. And as soon as they encounter a progressive school setting, it feels so right. A lot of parents can't express what they're looking for, but come to a school like ours and say, 'This is what I mean.' "

This may be a good time for me to remind those parents who have had trouble expressing what they're looking for, and teachers who have struggled to put into words what they are doing, of the definition I came up with on my travels to so many progressive schools. I hope it can help to clear up some of the awkwardness, as I've yet to read anything quite this concise or which captures our main goals in a way that has won agreement from so many of our leading members:

Progressive Education prepares students for active participation in a democratic society, in the context of a child-centered environment, and with an enduring commitment to social justice.

Truly, I hope it helps.

All that said, I now have one favor to ask before I leave these pages.

Can we please stop talking about Finland?

For one thing, our two nations are simply too different. Finland's population numbers barely 5.4 million people, less than 4 percent of whom live in poverty, and most of whom share with each other the same ethnic background and culture. Americans are fifty-eight times more numerous, dramatically more diverse, and, with nearly 22 percent living in poverty, far more economically and socially challenged.

When you compare apples to apples—our wealthiest schools to your average Finn classroom—we're doing just fine. Broaden your scope, however—to include the millions of American children suffering in substandard, dreary, punitive schools—and you'll realize we need to do much better. Of course, maybe Finland does show us the way, but only if you take into account that it's been our way all along. As Diane Ravitch has noted, Finland actually "borrowed" its main ideas from America, ideas that include equality of educational opportunity, individualized instruction, and cooperative learning. (Ravitch added, to my delight: "Most of its borrowing derives from the work of the philosopher John Dewey.") Finnish children enjoy educational benefits that progressive reformers have advocated for decades. They are free from mandated standardized tests, apart from one exam at the end of their senior year in high school. Competition between students, schools, and regions doesn't exist. Finnish teachers, moreover, are well trained, well paid, and given great freedom to determine how they do their jobs.

So, in other words, we could keep talking about Finland—and make ourselves miserable—or we can move forward, by reviving our own past. We have all the tools we need to make our education system great again. In fact, we invented them. Schools that produce bighearted innovators are part of our American heritage, and the time is ripe to share their benefits with many more American children.

EPILOGUE

A gazebo at Park Day School on the day after Tom Little's death.
Photograph courtesy of Cathy Shields

You made many changes in the world.
You taught us many things.
You were helpful and kind.
I am glad you lived a happy life. Thank you

A student's tribute to Tom Little. Photograph courtesy of Cathy Shields

Tom Little passed away on Tuesday, April 29, 2014.

It was less than three weeks after he had signed off on sending the manuscript of *Loving Learning* to his publisher.

When children arrived at Park Day School that Thursday, they saw the letters T-O-M painted in bold colors and surrounded by painted hearts on the pavement in front of the main school buildings. Elsewhere around campus, adults had painted the words "gratitude," "generosity," and "friend." Just after the morning dropoff, children, school staff members, and a few parents gathered on the field for ten minutes to hold hands, sing songs, and blow soap bubbles into the morning sunshine. Roughly five weeks later, a three-hour-long memorial service was held at the Berkeley Repertory Theater. The theater holds six hundred people, but so many former students and parents and teachers, including over thirty heads of other schools, and friends attended that some couldn't find empty seats.

Appendix

PROGRESSIVE EDUCATION ASSOCIATION:
SEVEN FOUNDING PRINCIPLES

In 1919, at the Washington, D.C., public library, a group of school founders and other reformers launched the Progressive Education Association. The members agreed on the following seven principles, which continue to comprise one of the best, if slightly unwieldy, descriptions of what makes Progressive Education distinct from conventional systems.

I. Freedom to Develop Naturally

The conduct of the pupil should be governed by himself according to the social needs of his community, rather than by arbitrary laws. Full opportunity for initiative and self-expression should be provided, together with an environment rich in interesting material that is available for the free use of every pupil.

II. Interest, the Motive of all Work

Interest should be satisfied and developed through: (1) Direct and indirect contact with the world and its activities, and use of the experience thus gained. (2) Application of knowledge gained, and correlation between different subjects. (3) The consciousness of achievement.

III. The Teacher a Guide, not a Task-Master

It is essential that teachers should believe in the aims and general principles of Progressive Education and that they should have latitude for the development of initiative and originality. Progressive teachers will encourage the use of all the senses, training the pupils in both observation and judgment; and instead of hearing recitations only, will spend most of the time teaching how to use various sources of information, including life activities as well as books; how to reason about the information thus acquired; and how to express forcefully and logically the conclusions reached. Ideal teaching conditions demand that classes be small, especially in the elementary school years.

IV. Scientific Study of Pupil Development

School records should not be confined to the marks given by the teachers to show the advancement of the pupils in their study of subjects, but should also include both objective and subjective reports on those physical, mental, moral and social characteristics which affect both school and adult life, and which can be influenced by the school and at home. Such records should be used as a guide for the treatment of each pupil, and should also serve to focus the attention of the teacher on the all-important work of development rather than on simply teaching subject matter.

V. Greater Attention to all that Affects the Child's Physical Development

One of the first considerations of Progressive Education is the health of the pupils. Much more room in which to move about, better light and air, clean and well ventilated buildings, easier access to the out-of-doors and greater use of it, are all necessary. There should be frequent use of adequate playgrounds. The teachers should observe closely the physical condition of each pupil and, in cooperation with the home, make abounding health the first objective of childhood.

VI. Co-operation Between School and Home to Meet the Needs of Child-Life

The school should provide, with the home, as much as is possible of all that the natural interests and activities of the child demand, especially during the elementary school years. These conditions can come about only through intelligent co-operation between parents and teachers.

VII. The Progressive School a Leader in Educational Movements

The Progressive School should be a leader in educational movements. It should be a laboratory where new ideas, if worthy, meet encouragement; where tradition alone does not rule, but the best of the past is leavened with the discoveries of today, and the result is freely added to the sum of educational knowledge.

We thank the Park School of Baltimore for listing these principles on their Web site.

A LIST OF SCHOOLS USING PROGRESSIVE EDUCATION METHODS

The schools listed below are either explicitly progressive or rely on key progressive methods, such as teaching to the "whole child."

Asterisks mark the names of the forty-five schools Tom Little visited for the purposes of this book.

Many of the entries are listed courtesy of film director Amy Valens, a retired Progressive Education elementary schoolteacher. Amy and her husband Tom co-produced the film *August to June.* They also produced *Good Morning Mission Hill,* a film about Mission Hill school in Boston. PEN boardmember Katy Dalgleish also helped gather names.

The list is by no means complete. It does not include Montessori and Waldorf schools, and many other schools that operate using progressive practices.

Alabama

Fairhope: The Murietta Johnson School of Organic Education

Alaska

Anchorage: Chugash Optional Elementary School

Arizona

Paradise Valley: The Tesseract School

California

*Altadena: Odyssey Charter School
*Berkeley: Berkwood Hedge School
Calabasas: Muse School
Camarillo: Camarillo Academy of Progressive Education
Campbell: Village School
Carmichael: Mission Avenue Open School
Chico: Hooker Oak Open Structured Classroom Program
———: Wildflower Open Classroom Public Charter School
Culver City: The Willows Community School
Danville: The Athenian School
Lawndale: Environmental Charter School
Long Beach: Chadwick School
———: New City Public Charter Schools
Los Altos: Ventana School
Los Angeles: Citizens of the World Charter Schools
———: The City School
———: The Oaks School
———: Open Magnet Charter School
———: UCLA Lab School

———: Vistamar School
———: Westland School
———: Westside Neighborhood School
*———: Wildwood School
Los Gatos: Hillbrook School
———: Mulberry School
Menlo Park: Peninsula School
Mountain View: Stevenson Elementary PACT
Napa: Blue Oak School
———: Vichy K–3 Alternative Elementary Program
North Hollywood: Oakwood School
Oakland: Aurora School
———: Park Day School
Palo Alto: Girls' Middle School
———: Mid-Peninsula High School
———: Ohlone Elementary School
*Pasadena: Sequoyah School
———: Walden School
———: The Waverly School
Petaluma: Mary Collins School at Cherry Valley
Redding: Chrysalis Charter School
Redwood City: Orion Alternative School
Richmond: Crestmont School
Salinas: Oasis Charter Public School
San Carlos: San Carlos Charter Learning Center
San Diego: Explorer Elementary Charter School
San Francisco: Children's Day School
———: Harvey Milk Civil Rights Academy
*———: Presidio Hill School
———: Rooftop Alternative School
———: Sanchez Elementary School
*———: San Francisco Friends School
———: Synergy School
———: The Urban School
San Geronimo: San Geronimo Open Classroom
*San Jose: Almaden Country School
———: Discovery Charter School 1
———: Discovery Charter School 2
———: Indigo School
Santa Barbara: Open Alternative School
Santa Clara: Washington Open Elementary
Santa Cruz: Gateway School
———: Monarch Community School
*Santa Monica: Crossroads School for Arts & Sciences
———: New Roads School

*———: PS 1 Pluralistic School
———: Santa Monica Alternative Schoolhouse
Saratoga: Christa McAuliffe School
*Van Nuys: Children's Community School
Ventura: Open Classroom
———: Ventura Charter School of Arts and Education

Colorado

Carbondale: Carbondale Community School Public Charter
———: Colorado Rocky Mountain School
Colorado Springs: Colorado Springs School
Estes Park: Eagle Rock School
Fort Collins: The Lab School
Frisco: The Peak School
Lakewood: Jefferson County Open School
Woody Hills: Aspen Community School Public Charter

Connecticut

Fairfield: The Unquowa School
Stamford: The Mead School

Georgia

Atlanta: The Galloway School
———: High Meadows
———: Paideia School

Hawaii

Honolulu: Iolani School
———: Punahou School

Illinois

*Berwyn: The Children's School
Chicago: Francis W. Parker School
*———: Namaste Charter School
———: The Nettlehorst School
*Wilmette: Baker Demonstration School
The Winnetka School District:
    *Greely School
    *Hubbard Woods Elementary School

Indiana

Chesterton: Discovery Charter
Indianapolis: Key Learning Community
*———: The Orchard School

Iowa

Iowa City: Willowwind School

Kansas

Wichita: Enders Open Magnet School

Kentucky

Goshen: St. Francis School
Louisville: Breckinridge-Franklin Elementary
———: Byck Elementary Magnet School

Maine

Alna: Juniper High School

Maryland

Baltimore: Creative City Charter
———: The Park School of Baltimore
———: Roots and Branches Charter School
*College Park: Friends Community School
*Rockville: Green Acres School

Massachussetts

Amherst: The Common School
*Boston: Mission Hill K–8 School
*Cambridge: Cambridge Friends School
*———: The Cambridge School of Weston
———: Fayerweather Street School
———: Graham and Parks Alternative School
———: King Open School
*———: Shady Hill School
Devins: Francis W. Parker Charter
Fitchburg: North Central Charter
Greenfield: Center School
Springfield: Rebecca Johnson School

Michigan

Ann Arbor: Ann Arbor Open School
Ferndale: John F. Kennedy School Open Classroom
Grand Haven: The Voyager School, Ferry Elementary

Minnesota

Minneapolis: Clara Barton Open School
———: Marcy Open School

Northfield: Prairie Creek Community School
St. Paul: Friends School of Minnesota
————: Open World Learning Community

Missouri

St. Louis: The College School of Webster Groves
————: The Community School
————: New City School
————: Whitfield School

New Hampshire

Amherst: Souhegan High School
Harrisville: Wells Memorial School
Manchester: Making Connections Charter (MC2)
Surrey: Surrey Village Charter

New Jersey

Farmingdale: Voyagers' Community School
Montclair: Montclair Cooperative School

New York

*Buffalo: The Park School of Buffalo (Snyder, NY)
Ithaca: Lehman Alternative Community School
Mt. Vernon: Lincoln Elementary

New York City

The Bronx: Bronx Community Charter School
————: Bronx Little School
Brooklyn: Bedford Stuyvesant New Beginnings Charter School
————: Brooklyn Free School
————: Brooklyn Friends School
————: Brooklyn New School, PS 146
————: Community Roots Charter School
————: Compass Charter School
————: Greene Hill School
————: International School of Brooklyn
Manhattan: Avenues: The World School
*————: Bank Street School for Children
————: Battery Park City School
————: Beacon High School
————: The Blue School
*————: Calhoun School
————: Castle Bridge School, PS 513
————: Central Park East I, PS 467

———: Central Park East II, PS 964
———: The Charrette School, PS 3
———: Chelsea Day School
———: Children's Workshop School
*———: City and Country School
———: Corlears School
———: Dalton School
———: The Earth School
———: East Village Community School
———: Elizabeth Irwin High School
———: Ella Baker School
*———: Ethical Culture Fieldston School
———: Freebrook Academy
———: Harlem Link Charter School
*———: Independence School, PS 234
*———: Little Red School House
*———: Manhattan Country School
———: Manhattan New School
———: Manhattan School for Children
———: Muscota New School, PS 314
———: Neighborhood School, PS 363
———: The New Vision School, PS 69
*———: The School at Columbia University
———: School of the Future
———: Urban Academy Laboratory High School
———: *William T. Sherman School, PS 87
———: Village Community School
*Poughkeepsie: Poughkeepsie Day School
Southold: Peconic Community School
Wappingers Falls: The Randolph School

North Carolina

Davidson: Community School of Davidson
Durham: Carolina Friends School
———: The Duke School
Harrisburg: Bradley Preparatory School
Winston-Salem: Arts Based Elementary

Ohio

Columbus: Douglas Alternative Elementary School
Hilliard: Alton Darby Elementary
Stewart: Federal Hocking High School
*Upper Arlington: Wickliffe Progressive Community School

Oregon

Eugene: Camas Ridge Community School
————: Corridor Alternative Elementary
————: Family School
Portland: Arbor School of Arts and Sciences
————: Catlin Gabel School
————: Opal Charter School

Pennsylvania

*Conshohocken: The Miquon School
*Philadelphia: The Philadelphia School
*————: The Crefeld School
*Rose Valley: The School in Rose Valley

Utah

Salt Lake City: Salt Lake City Open Classroom Charter

Vermont

*Putney: Putney School
Sharon: Sharon Academy
Westminster: Compass School
————: Westminster Community School

Virginia

*Alexandria: Burgundy Farm Country Day School
Fairfax: Mantua Elementary School
Free Union: Free Union Country School

Washington

Bellevue: The Little School
Seattle: The Bush School
————: Salmon Bay School
————: Thornton Creek School
————: University Cooperative School

Washington, DC

*Capitol Hill Day School
Georgetown Day School
*Lowell School
*Sheridan School
*Sidwell Friends School

Wisconsin

Green Bay: Aldo Leopold Community School
Madison: Open Classroom at Lincoln
*————: Wingra School
Milwaukee: La Escuela Fratney

A (SOMEWHAT IDIOSYNCRATIC) TOP-TEN LIST OF BOOKS, STUDIES, AND ARTICLES SUPPORTING THE BENEFITS OF PROGRESSIVE EDUCATION

1. Joseph Watras, *The Eight-Year Study: From Evaluative Research to a Demonstration Project, 1930–1940.* Education Policy Analysis Archives.

2. *How People Learn: Brain, Mind, Experience, and School.* National Research Council, 2000. National Academy Press.

3. Stuart Brown and Christian Vaughan, *Play: How It Shapes the Brain, Opens the Imagination, and Invigorates the Soul.* Avery Trade; April 6, 2010.

4. Clea A. McNeely, James M. Nonnemaker, and Robert W. Blum, "Promoting School Connectedness: Evidence from the National Longitudinal Study of Adolescent Health," *Journal of School Health* (2002).

5. "Social-Emotional Learning," *From Practice to Policy.* National Association of State Boards of Education, vol. 1, no. 1 (October 2013).

6. Vanessa Vega, "Project-Based Learning Research Review," *Edutopia,* Dec. 3, 2012.

7. Louis Cozolino, "Nine Things Educators Need to Know About the Brain," *Greater Good,* Mar. 19, 2003.

8. Helen Y. Weng et al., "Compassion Training Alters Altruism and Neural Responses to Suffering," *Psychological Science,* vol. 24, no. 7 (2013), 1171–80.

9. Ron Berger, *An Ethic of Excellence.* William Heinemann, 2003.

10. Kelly Lambert, *Lifting Depression: A Neuroscientist's Hands-on Approach to Activating Your Brain's Healing Power.* Basic Books, 2010.

PARK DAY SCHOOL'S SIXTH-GRADERS' POEM TO TOM LITTLE

Tom

Tom is a sage, wise owl
sitting atop an ancient oak tree
watching a vivid sunset.

He is an old fountain pen
dancing nimbly across a piece of paper
inking out ideas for a better world.

Tom is one of those warm rainy days
where everyone is splashing in puddles
and spinning around trying to catch the raindrops.

He is a radiant red apple
hanging off a tree
glistening in the sunlight.

He is a summer morning
waking everyone up
greeting them.

Tom is a huge magnolia tree
with large leaves
shading the entire school.

Notes

INTRODUCTION: MEET ME AT PARK DAY

16 **More than 1.3 million American students drop out**: In 2014, U.S. high school graduation rates reached a modern record of 80 percent, which was good news, although big problems and disparities continue. See Lyndsey Layton, "High School Graduation Rates at Historic High," *Washington Post*, Apr. 28, 2014; and "Study: Just Over Half of College Graduates Complete Degrees," *Time*, Dec. 16, 2013, http://nation.time.com/2013/12/16/study-just-over-half-of-college-students-complete-degrees/.

16 **U.S. teens have ranked twenty-fifth among thirty-four industrialized nations**: "U.S. Students Still Lag Behind Foreign Peers, Schools Make Little Progress in Improving Achievement," *Huffington Post*, July 7, 2012.

16 **Student morale is in equally dismal shape**: "National Study: Teen Misuse and Abuse of Prescription Drugs Up 33 Percent Since 2008, Stimulants Contributing to Sustained Rx Epidemic," Apr. 22, 2013, http://www.drugfree.org/newsroom/national-study-teen-misuse-and-abuse-of-prescription-drugs-up-33-percent-since-2008-stimulants-contributing-to-sustained-rx-epidemic/.

28 **In recent years, Silicon Valley moguls**: Frank DiGiacomo, "School for Cool," *Vanity Fair* (March 2005); "Valley School Named After Schwarzenegger," *Los Angeles Daily News*, Nov. 21, 2010.

30 **Nor was Obama, at least initially, a model student**: Barack Obama, *Dreams from My Father* (New York: Crown, 1995); Carlyn Tani, "A Kid Called Barry," *Punahou Bulletin* (Spring 2007).

CHAPTER 1: "REMAKERS OF MANKIND"

33 **And *Emile* had a tremendous impact**: Kant's tribute is noted in Dieter Henrich, *Between Kant and Hegel: Lectures on German Idealism* (Cambridge, MA: Harvard University Press, 2003).

34   **learning by "heart, head, and hand"**: Michel Soëtard, "Johann Hein-rich Pestalozzi (1746–1827)," *Quarterly Review of Comparative Education* (Paris: UNESCO, International Bureau of Education), vol. XXIV, no. 1/2 (1994), 297–310.

34   **As urban populations increased**: The school attendance statistic comes from the Fourteenth Census of the United States Taken in the Year 1920 (Washington, DC: U.S. Bureau of the Census, Vol. 5).

35   **"That there was need for the reaction, indeed for a revolt"**: Dewey is cited in Stephen G. Weiss, Anthony deFalco, and Eileen M. Weiss, "Progessive=Permissive? Not According to John Dewey: Subjects Matter!" 2005, http://www.usca.edu/essays/vol142005/defalco.pdf.

35   **The dismal state of so many of the common schools**: Joseph M. Rice, *The Public-School System of the United States* (New York: Century Publ., 1893).

36   **While determinedly chronicling the worst of public education**: Lawrence A. Cremin, *The Transformation of the School* (New York: Vintage Books, 1964).

38   **"a model home, a complete community"**: Ibid., p. 132.

39   **Montessori schools**: Jim Powell, "Maria Montessori, Who Gave Children Everywhere Freedom to Achieve Independence," *The Freeman*, Aug. 1, 1995, and Jim Powell, *Maria Montessori: A Biography*, Radcliffe Biography Series (Cambridge, MA: Da Capo Press, 1988). For a look at the many similarities between American progressive and Montessori schools, see this chart: *Bright Horizons Educational Programs: Comparing Montessori and Progressive Methods,* at http://beta.brookfieldacademy.net/beta/montessori_slick_2_FINAL.pdf.

40   **It's striking that long before the age**: Yong Zhao, a professor at the University of Oregon College of Education, grew up in China and experienced its education system as both a student and a teacher. In his *Catching Up or Leading the Way* (2009), he elucidates one of the great ironies of the current model of American schooling. As he writes: "China is determined to transform from a labor-intensive, low-level manufacturing economy into an innovation-driven knowledge society. . . . Thus China decided to change its 'test-oriented education' into 'talent-oriented education.' To engineer this change, China made a conscious, global search for models—education systems that are good at producing innovative talents. As a country with the most Nobel Laureates, most original patents, most scientific discoveries in the twentieth century, and largest economy in the world, the United States of America seems a reasonable candidate."

Another interesting reference to progressive schools in China is Ian Johnson's, "A Waldorf School in China," *The New Yorker,* Jan. 27, 2014.

41   **"If I should tell you any secret"**: Cremin, *The Transformation of the School,* p. 128.

41   **making school more like "real life"**: Katherine Camp Edwards, *The Dewey School: The Laboratory School of the University of Chicago 1896–1903* (New York: D. Appleton-Century Co., 1936).

42   **"tiny and, in many eyes, a crackpot movement"**: "Education: Progressives' Progress," *Time,* Oct. 31, 1938.

42   **A few years later, the movement gained considerable prestige**: Joseph Watras, "The Eight-Year Study: From Evaluative Research to a Demonstration Project, 1930–1940," Education Policy Analysis Archives, http://epaa.asu.edu/ojs/article/view/92.

43   **"really stupid . . . it misconceives the conditions of independent thinking"**: Jerry Kirkpatrick, *Montessori, Dewey, and Capitalism: Educational Theory for a Free Market in Education* (New York: TLJ Books, 2008).

44   **"the errand boys of big business"**: "Dr. John Dewey Dead at 92," *New York Times,* June 2, 1952.

44   **making U.S. education "effeminate"**: "Education: Progressives' Progress," cited above. Another major critic, the academic historian Arthur Bestor, charged in his *Educational Wastelands* (1953) that progressive educators had "lowered the aims of the American public schools" by "setting forth purposes for education so trivial as to forfeit the respect of thoughtful men, and by deliberately divorcing the schools from the disciplines of science and scholarship."

45   **"I walk into that so-called"**: Patrick Dennis, *Auntie Mame: An Irreverent Escapade* (New York: Broadway Books, 2001).

46   **"Just as the biologist can take"**: John Dewey, "The School and Society and the Child and the Curriculum," Digireads.com Publishing, Jan. 1, 2010, p. 15.

48   **I started graduate school in the mid-1970s**: See Larry Cuban, "The Open Classroom: Were Schools Without Walls Just Another Fad?" *Education Next,* vol. 4, no. 2 (2004), p. 68–71.

50   **"None exists, and none ever will"**: Cremin, *The Transformation of the School,* p. x.

CHAPTER 2: THE RUG

56 **In 1928, Mary Hammett Lewis**: Mary Hammett Lewis, *An Adventure with Children* (Buffalo, NY: The Park School, 2011).

60 **Unfortunately, many children report feeling chronically over-stressed**: David Ruenzel, "Why Zebras Don't Get Ulcers," *Brain Connection*, Mar. 12, 2003.

62 **Plenty of additional evidence supports the benefits**: Clea A. McNeely, James M. Nonnemaker, and Robert W. Blum, "Promoting School Connectedness: Evidence from the National Longitudinal Study of Adolescent Health," *Journal of School Health* (2002).

65 **The conservative English philosopher Michael Oakeshott**: Michael Oakeshott, "Education: The Engagement and Its Frustration," *Journal of Philosophy of Education*, vol. 5, no. 1 (January 1971), 43–76.

66 **in a landmark study launched in Tennessee**: Frederick Mosteller, "The Tennessee Study of Class Size in the Early School Grades," *Critical Issues for Children and Youths*, vol. 5, no. 2 (Summer–Fall 1995). The benefits of smaller student-teacher ratios in fact have become such conventional wisdom that Malcolm Gladwell recently challenged the idea in his book *Goliath*. Gladwell noted that some research shows that many teachers assigned to small classrooms simply choose to work less, rather than adjust their teaching styles in ways that would benefit their students. Yet while this may be true in some conventional schools—and especially those where teachers with impossible workloads may be desperate for any free moments they can cadge—progressive teachers not only usually work under more humane conditions but are trained to have students do more independent and group work, with more one-on-one meetings with teachers, techniques that ensure the advantages of the smaller classrooms.

66 **more than 300,000 teachers nationwide**: *Investing in Our Future: Returning Teachers to the Classroom* (August 2012).

CHAPTER 3: THE INNER EAR

74 **"Why should they look behind"**: Cremin, *The Transformation of the School*, p. 5.

75 **"We're teaching the child"**: Peter Gray quoted in Joshua Davis, "How a Radical New Teaching Method Could Unleash a Generation of Geniuses," *Wired*, Nov. 2013, 160, http://www.wired.com/2013/10/free-thinkers/all/.

76 **"The model of the child as an empty vessel"**: National Research

Council, *How People Learn: Brain, Mind, Experience, and School* (Washington, DC: National Academies Press, 2000). The report was produced by five editors belonging to the Council's committees on Developments in the Science of Learning and Learning Research and Educational Practices.

77 **"How a Radical New Teaching Method Could Unleash a Generation of Geniuses"**: Joshua Davis, *Wired*, Oct. 15, 2013.

78 **The most important of their founding principles**: S. P. Chaube, *Foundations of Education* (Kolkata, Uttar Pradesh: Vikas Publishing House Pvt Ltd., 2009).

78 **play is a ramp to joyful learning**: As it happens, the keynote speaker at the PEN Conference in Los Angeles was Stuart Brown, a medical researcher who has based his career on the benefits of play, as the founder of the National Institute for Play and author of *Play: How It Shapes the Brain, Opens the Imagination, and Invigorates the Soul* (2010). Brown and other scientists warn of what they describe as a sharp recent decline in the amount of time children these days have available to play, and of a culture so hell-bent on constant achievement that we're drilling academics into kids as soon as they start kindergarten.

80 **researchers have found that it is just these students who stand to benefit most**: These findings and others appeared in a report titled *Arts Education in Public Elementary and Secondary Schools: 2009–10* (National Center for Education Statistics, 2012).

81 **students who took four years of art and music classes**: *College-Bound Seniors: Total Group Profile Report* (New York: The College Board, 2007). The study also found that students who took four years of arts and music classes while in high school scored 91 points better on their SAT exams than students who took only a half year or less.

83 **Joan Wright-Albertini's annual ecosystem unit**: This description is based on an interview with Ms. Albertini and a write-up in Lisa Bennett and Daniel Goleman, *Ecoliterate: How Educators Are Cultivating Emotional, Social, and Ecological Intelligence* (San Francisco: Jossey-Bass, 2012).

86 **One widely cited study**: J. Boaler, "Equity, Empowerment and Different Ways of Knowing," *Mathematics Education Research Journal*, vol. 9, no. 3 (1997), 325–42.

86 **project-based learning will be key**: Vanessa Vega, "Project-Based Learning Research Review," *Edutopia*, Dec. 3, 2012.

88 **In a classic study of the so-called Pygmalion effect**: Robert Rosenthal and Lenore Jacobson, "Pygmalion in the Classroom," *Urban Review* (September 1968).

CHAPTER 4: THE MAGIC CIRCLE

94 **The number of high school students suspended or expelled**: Robert K. Ross and Kenneth H. Zimmerman, "Real Discipline in School," *New York Times,* Feb. 16, 2014. In 2012, the Council of State Governments Justice Center, a non-profit policy group, issued a study of policies in Texas showing that nearly six in ten public school students had been suspended or expelled at least once between seventh and twelfth grades, with only a tiny percentage for cases involving serious criminal conduct.

94 **a long article extolling the art of collaboration**: In fact, the *Harvard Business Review* has published several major stories on this topic, compiled in a 2013 book, *HBR's 10 Must Reads on Collaboration*, http://www.amazon.com/Collaboration-featured-Intelligence-Leadership-Boyatzis/dp/1422190129.

95 **his goal of creating "social-mindedness" in children**: Carleton Washburne, *What Is Progressive Education?* (New York: John Day Co., 1952), p. 22.

97 **"The Five Habits of Mind"**: Deborah Meier, *The Power of Their Ideas: Lessons for America from a Small School in Harlem* (Boston: Beacon Press, 1995).

99 **A textbook case**: Corey Kilgannon, "Doctor Saves an African Boy, and Vice Versa; Brought to New York for Care, an Orphan Transforms His Benefactor's Life," *New York Times*, May 30, 2003.

101 **from truancy to graffiti to bullying**: Peter Gray, "School Bullying: A Tragic Cost of Undemocratic Schools," Psychology Today.com, May 12, 2010.

102 **"Mr. Dobbin's lashings"**: Mark Twain, *The Adventures of Tom Sawyer* (New York: 1876; Harper & Bros., 1903), http://twain.lib.virginia.edu/tomsawye/text/TS21.html.

105 **a 14 percent drop in suspensions**: Ross and Zimmerman, "Real Discipline in School," *New York Times*, Feb. 16, 2014.

106 **girls by many measures are outperforming boys**: Lesley Stahl, "The Gender Gap: Boys Lagging," CBS, *60 Minutes*, Oct. 31, 2002.

106 **a mention on the front page of the *New York Times***: http://www.nytimes.com/2006/12/02/us/02child.html?pagewanted=all&_r=0.

107 **"This is different"**: Brill says she doesn't believe the numbers of trans-gender children are increasing, contending that they may merely seem more numerous due to changing attitudes that have allowed for more openness. Sadly, I wonder if the increased amount of environmental exposure to endocrine disruptors may also be playing a role.

109 **We got ribbed a little**: Meredith May, "Teaching the reality of gay life / Oakland schoolkids learn a rare lesson," *San Francisco Chronicle*, Mar. 10, 2002.

111 **"Everything I do is visible"**: Some quotes by Gavins were reported in Sam Chaltain, "Mission (Upon a) Hill," *Democracy. Learning. Voice*, Feb. 20, 2012, http://www.samchaltain.com/stories-of-transformation -mission-upon-a-hill.

CHAPTER 5: THE STORYBOARD

118 **the effectiveness of computers in the classroom**: H. Wenglinsky, *Does It Compute? The Relationship Between Educational Technology and Student Achievement in Mathematics* (Princeton, NJ: Policy Information Center of the Educational Testing Service, 1998).

119 **students doubled their class average**: B. Penuel et al., *Silicon Valley Challenge 2000: Year 5 Multimedia Project Report* (Menlo Park, CA: SRI International, 2001).

121 **"Technology is just a tool"**: Keith Upchurch, "Gates: Tech just tool for making human connections," *Herald Sun* (Durham, NC), May 12, 2003.

123 **"Makers are in a position to understand and change the world"**: Tremayne quoted in Stett Holbrook, "Making Makers at the East Bay Mini Maker Faire," *Make*, Oct. 20, 2013.

124 **less vulnerable to depression**: For a whole book on this topic, see Kelly Lambert's *Lifting Depression: A Neuroscientist's Hands-On Approach to Activating Your Brain's Healing Power* (New York: Basic Books, 2008).

126 **As its former principal Grace Rotzel explained**: Grace Rotzel, *The School in Rose Valley* (New York: Ballantine Books, 1972), p. 19.

127 **As Chubb wrote in a blog**: John Chubb, "Student Choice and Classrooms of the Future," National Association of Independent Schools, Feb. 2, 2014.

CHAPTER 6: TASTING THE SOUP

131 **ticking off statistics about mental disorders**: See "School Drug Use: Survey Finds 17 Percent of High School Students Drink, Smoke, Use

Drugs During the School Day," *Huffington Post*, Aug. 23, 2012; and Robert Kolker, "Cheating Upwards," *New York Magazine*, Sept. 16, 2012.

131 **suicide continues to be the third leading cause of death**: "U.S.A. Suicide: 2010 Official Final Data, American Association of Suicidology," http://mypage.iusb.edu/~jmcintos; Maria L. La Ganga, "Palo Alto Campus Searches for Healing After Suicides," *Los Angeles Times*, Oct. 30, 2009. There is more bad news that Levine hasn't even mentioned, but that we've all been hearing through our networks. For instance, studies of tens of thousands of children have shown that the average U.S. schoolchild in recent decades has been reporting levels of anxiety higher than the average psychiatric patient of the 1950s: http://www.apa.org/news/press/releases/2000/12/anxiety.aspx.

132 **they get barely fifteen minutes**: Eric Westervelt, "These Days, School Lunch Hours Are More Like 15 Minutes," NPR, "The Salt," Dec. 4, 2013.

132 **"unhurried by those who are quicker"**: William Meuer and Jan Tubergen, Winnetka Historical Society (originally publ. 1998), http://winnetkahistory.org/gazette/carleton-washburne/.

133 **the Badass Teachers Association (BAT)**: "The Rise of the Badass Teachers Association—A Brief History," from the blog *With a Brooklyn Accent*, Oct. 20, 2013.

134 **"testing mania"**: "The Trouble with Testing Mania," *New York Times*, Editorial Board, July 13, 2013.

134 **big awkward "X's" through the problems**: Valerie Strauss, "A Ridiculous Common Core Test for First Graders," *Washington Post*, Oct. 31, 2013.

137 **abysmal levels of student preparedness**: Justin Doubleday, "Most Students Are Unprepared for College, SAT Results Show," *Chronicle of Higher Education*, Sept. 26, 2013.

140 **more like "rigor mortis"**: Alfie Kohn, *Punished by Rewards: The Trouble with Gold Stars, Incentive Plans, A's, Praise, and Other Bribes* (New York: Mariner Books, Houghton Mifflin Harcourt, 1999).

143 **Consider Casco Bay High School**: Casco's instruction approach is explained in more detail at http://cbhs.portlandschools.org/files/2011/04/CBHS-School-Profile-2013-14.pdf.

147 **A RAND Corporation report**: *Measuring 21st-century Competencies. Guidance for Educators*, RAND Corporation, November 2013. Among the schools I visited in 2013 were three that used this test: Almaden in San Jose; Sidwell Friends in Washington, DC; and Shady Hill School in Cambridge, MA.

CHAPTER 7: THE LABORATORY

150 **"Do you call this a school?"**: Caroline Pratt, *I Learn from Children* (New York: Grove Press, 2014), p. 3.

151 **"I began to see education"**: Petra Munro Henry, "Learning from Caroline Pratt," *Journal of the American Association for the Advancement of Curriculum Studies*, 4 (February 2008), http://www2.uwstout.edu /content/jaaacs/vol4/hendry.pdf.

151 **"All my life I have fought"**: Ibid.

153 **"nothing was fixed"**: Ibid.

153 **"License began to pass"**: Cremin, *The Transformation of the School*, p. 207.

154 **"free-range childhood"**: Matthew Appleton, *A Free Range Childhood: Self-Regulation at Summerhill School*, Foundation for Educational Renewal, Jan. 1, 2000.

154 **"No one is wise enough"**: A. S. Neill, *Summerhill—A Radical Approach to Education* (London: Victor Gollancz, 1966), n.p.

156 **The notion formally arose in a 1945 report by the Department of Education**: See Cremin, *The Transformation of the School*, p. 335.

CHAPTER 8: THE PETITION

169 **Barely 41 percent of voters**: Furthermore, half of all potential voters ages 18–29 are not registered to vote, which is the lowest rate in the past sixteen years of Pew Research Center's polling—Clare Malone, "Young, Restless, and Not Voting," *American Prospect*, Apr. 26, 2012.

169 **only 19 percent of Millennials**: Charles M. Blow, "The Self(ie) Generation," *New York Times*, Mar. 7, 2014.

170 **On a visit to his alma mater**: Tani, "A Kid Called Barry," *Punahou Bulletin* (Spring 2007).

171 **people of all ages are more motivated to learn**: Helen Y. Weng et al., "Compassion Training Alters Altruism and Neural Responses to Suffering," *Psychological Science*, vol. 24, no. 7 (2013), 1171–80; and B. J. S. Barron et al., with The Cognition and Technology Group at Vanderbilt, "Doing with Understanding: Lessons from Research on Problem- and Project-Based Learning," *Journal of the Learning Sciences*, vol. 7 (1998), 271–311.

174 **"It takes thirty-nine people to make a coat"**: Addams quoted in Cremin, *The Transformation of the School*, p. 62.

174 **"The ideal of the school"**: Jared Stallones, "Conflict and Resolution: Progressive Educators and the Question of Religion," Information Age Publishing (2010), 49.

177 **In many other cases, our choice of location reflects our strong environmental values**: Without substantial investments, the majority of our urban schools include some sort of gardening program, even if it only involves small raised beds plopped on asphalt playgrounds. Many make a point of having students help raise produce for their lunches.

178 **To Jennifer Morgan-Bennett**: Jennifer Morgan-Bennett, "Sliding Scale Tuition and Our Family," November 2011, http://www.manhattan countryschool.org/sites/manhattancountryschool.org/files/FutureOf MCS-SlidingScaleTuition.pdf.

180 **"We don't have a crisis in education"**: Lloyd Vries, "Where's Iraq? Young Adults Don't Know," CBS/AP, May 2, 2006.

CONCLUSION: BACK TO THE FUTURE

192 **Those of us who believe that the Common Core represents at least potential progress**: Jay McTighe and Grant Wiggins in *Understanding by Design* have written that "Merely trying to retrofit the Standards to typical teaching and testing practices will undermine the effort"; http://grantwiggins.files.wordpress.com/2012/09/mctighe_wiggins_ final_common_core_standards.pdf.

192 **In a 2011 column for *Edutopia***: See http://www.edutopia.org /blog/learning-funnel-design-meaningful-work-elliot-washor-charles -mojkowski.

193 **Today, it boasts forty-four schools**: A recent report has shown that Big Picture's educational model outperforms its peers. In 2009, thirty-one Big Picture schools in eighteen school districts had higher graduation rates (92%) than the equivalent district rate (74%). For its California schools, evaluators found that Big Picture schools had substantially lower dropout rates and better academic performance among disadvantaged students. Three quarters of Big Picture students enroll in college. See "Spotlight On: Big Picture Learning," The Stuart Foundation, http://www.stuartfoundation.org/OurStrategy/Education Systems/TeachingandLearning/SpotlightonBigPictureLearning.

194 **schools using its model consistently outperform district averages**: In *Comprehensive School Reform and Student Achievement: A Meta-Analysis* (2002), researchers from the University of Wisconsin, Johns Hopkins University, and the University of North Carolina studied twenty-nine models of comprehensive school reform, including Expeditionary

Learning. Only three of the twenty-nine other models received higher ratings.

195 **and run by four progressive schools**: The four schools are the Calhoun School in Manhattan, the Cambridge School of Weston, the Putney School in Vermont, and Unquowa School in Connecticut. These specialized programs add to ongoing work by progressive faculty at institutions including U.C. Berkeley (the Developmental Teacher Education Program); Lesley College and its partnership with Shady Hill School; Michigan State University in Ann Arbor and its close association with Jay Featherstone; Mills College in Oakland, CA; Ohio State University in Columbus, OH; and Pacific Oaks College in Santa Monica, CA.

196 **the LinkedIn co-founder Reid Hoffman**: "How I Did It: Reid Hoffman of LinkedIn," *Inc.*, http://www.inc.com/magazine/20090501/how-i-did-it-reid-hoffman-of-linkedin.html.

197 **Several schools ... have already stopped explicitly calling themselves progressive**: And then there are the books—so many recently that champion teaching methods straight from Dewey, Parker, and Pratt, yet usually without mentioning that legacy. Just one example, *An Ethic of Excellence*, by Ron Berger, published in 2003, details several quintessentially progressive teaching methods, including students supporting one another through critique and deep analysis; the expectations that students create multiple drafts and iterations of their work; making student work public and celebrated; bringing the "real world," as Berger puts it, into the classroom regularly; multiple ways of assessment that are formative and ongoing; and holding students to the highest possible expectations. Like progressive educators, Berger believes and trusts in the capacity of his students to do remarkable things. You could take his class and plunk it down in a progressive school anywhere in the country and hardly anyone would know the difference. Yet nowhere in his book does he use the word "progressive." It is as though the concept has left our collective memory.

199 **"Who gets this?"**: "Lou Gehrig's famous speech," MLB.com, June 18, 2003.

203 **Finland actually "borrowed" its main ideas**: See Diane Ravitch, "Schools We Can Envy," *New York Review of Books*, Mar. 8, 2012; and LynNell Hancock, "Why are Finland's Schools So Successful?" *Smithsonian Magazine* (September 2011).

Bibliography

Ayers, Rick and William (2011). *Teaching the Taboo: Courage and Imagination in the Classroom*. New York & London: Teachers College Press.

Beilock, Sian (2010). *Choke: What the Secrets of the Brain Reveal About Getting It Right When You Have To*. New York: Atria Books.

Bode, H. Boyd (1938). *Progressive Education at the Crossroads*. New York: Newson & Co.

Brown, Stuart (2010). *Play: How It Shapes the Brain, Opens the Imagination, and Invigorates the Soul*. New York: Penguin Books, Avery.

Carbone, Peter F. Jr. (1977). *The Social and Educational Thought of Harold Rugg*. Durham, NC: Duke University Press.

Cremin, Lawrence A. (1961). *The Transformation of the School: Progressivism in American Education, 1876–1957*. New York: Vintage Books.

Cunitz, Daniel A., Sara Narva, and George Zeleznik (2011). *Progressive Education: The Advisory Program*. Philadelphia: Crefeld Publishing.

Damrosch, Leo (2005). *Jean-Jacques Rousseau: Restless Genius*. Boston & New York: Houghton Mifflin Co.

Dewey, John (1902). *The Child and the Curriculum*. Chicago: University of Chicago Press.

———— (1902). *The School and Society*. Chicago: University of Chicago Press.

———— (1909). *Moral Principles in Education*. London: Arcturus Books.

———— (1913). *Interest and Effort in Education*. Cambridge, MA: Riverside Press.

———— (1916). *Democracy and Education*. New York: Free Press.

———— (1938). *Experience and Education*. New York: Free Press.

Engel, Brenda S., with Anne C. Matine, eds. (2005). *Holding Values: What We Mean by Progressive Education*. Portsmouth, NH: William Heinemann.

Ginsburg, Herbert, and Sylvia Opper (1969). *Piaget's Theory of Intellectual Development: An Introduction*. Englewood Cliffs, NJ: Prentice-Hall.

Gray, Peter (2013). *Free to Learn: Why Unleashing the Instinct to Play Will Make Our Children Happier, More Self-Reliant, and Better Students for Life*. New York: Basic Books.

Halaby, Mona (2000). *Belonging: Creating Community in the Classroom.* Northampton, MA: Brookline Books.

Hofstadter, Richard (1963). *The Progressive Movement: 1900 to 1915.* New York: Simon & Schuster.

Jervis, Kathe, and Arthur Tobier (1987). *Education for Democracy. Proceedings from The Cambridge School Conference on Progressive Education.* Cambridge, MA: The Cambridge School.

Kilpatrick, William Heard (1918). *The Project Method: The Use of the Purposeful Act in the Education Process.* Whitefish, MT: Kessinger Publishing.

——— (1925). *Foundations of Method—Informal Talks on Teaching.* New York: The Macmillan Company.

Knoester, Matthew (2012). *Democratic Education in Practice: Inside the Mission Hill School.* New York: Teachers College Press.

Kohn, Alfie (1998). *What to Look For in a Classroom.* San Francisco: Jossey-Bass.

——— (2004). *What Does It Mean to Be Well Educated?* Boston: Beacon Press.

——— (2014). *The Myth of the Spoiled Child: Challenging the Conventional Wisdom About Children and Parenting.* Cambridge, MA: Da Capo Press.

Kozol, Jonathan (1985). *Death at an Early Age.* New York: Plume.

Levine, Madeline (2008). *The Price of Privilege.* New York: Harper Perennial.

Platt, Caroline (1948/2014). *I Learn from Children.* New York: Grove Press.

Rathbone, Charles H. (2008). *Fayerweather at 40.* Cambridge, MA: Harvard University Press.

Ravitch, Diane (1983). *The Troubled Crusade. American Education, 1945–1980.* New York: Basic Books.

Rotzel, Grace (1972). *The School in Rose Valley.* New York: Ballantine Books.

Ryan, Alan (1995). *John Dewey and the High Tide of American Liberalism.* New York: W. W. Norton & Co.

Semel, Susan F., and Alan R. Sadovnik, eds. (1999). *"Schools of Tomorrow," Schools of Today: What Happened to Progressive Education?* New York: Peter Lang.

———, eds. (2002). *Founding Mothers and Others: Women Educational Leaders During the Progressive Era.* New York: Palgrave.

Walkerdine, Valerie (1990). *Schoolgirl Fictions.* London & New York: Verso Books.

Washburne, Carleton (1952). *What Is Progressive Education? A Book for Parents and Others.* New York: John Day Company.

Whitehead, Alfred North (1929). *The Aims of Education and Other Essays.* New York: Free Press.

Acknowledgments

Tom Little: This book has been a dream for a very long time. Rather quietly, many years ago, I shared my dream with a friend. Though the years passed, she remembered the dream, and because of her generosity and kindness, the dream is now a reality. I will begin my acknowledgments and thanks by expressing the deepest gratitude to Michelle Mercer and her husband, Bruce Golden, who supported my project all along the way. Michelle and Bruce sponsored the sabbatical leave that allowed me to travel around the country studying Progressive Education, and then the subsequent hiring of Katherine Ellison, from whom I received writing support after completing the initial manuscript. Because of my current health situation, it would not have been possible for me to complete this work, and I am forever indebted to Michelle and Bruce for their generosity, friendship, love, and caring.

My assistant at Park Day School, Siobhan Cassidy, was with me each step along the way and coordinated my tour in advance, ensuring that there would be no glitches or interruptions, and indeed, the tour was flawless. I am enormously grateful to her.

I have been the fortunate recipient of support from my friend and former board chair, Frances Dinkelspiel, who all throughout the project has contributed her keen writer's eye and candid feedback to the manuscript. Beyond that, though, she has been unconditionally encouraging. My friends and professional colleagues, Maureen Cheever and Katy Dalgleish, helped me establish and maintain our aspiration to pursue an academic tone for the project and make it substantive for the teaching and learning community. As veteran progressive educators, their eyes have been invaluable. Thanks also to Dan Schwartz and Lisa Shapiro for their ongoing contributions.

Sincere appreciation to our literary agent, Bonnie Nadell, who so enthusiastically adopted this project and led us to submitting a winning proposal. And to Amy Cherry, our editor and wonderful collaborator at Norton—who would have guessed that the book would find a progressive publisher?

I have been working at Park Day School for almost forty years, where I have been allowed to grow, learn, and pursue my passions. I want to thank Heather Kuiper, the chair of the Board of Directors, who supported my project from the beginning, always with an optimistic and positive outlook on the work. I also want to thank the Park Day School staff for their encouragement and participation in the project, particularly Cathy Shields, John Orbon, Susan Erb, Harriet Cohen, Suzann Grody, Maria Montes Clemens, Mona Halaby, and Bob Rollins. Thanks to Flo Hodes for her unheralded anchoring of the school during these challenging times. I want to convey all best wishes to Jon Kidder as the school transitions to the future.

Close to the Park Day School community are Jonathan Berk and Rebecca Schwartz. I thank them for their ideas, encouragement, meals, and friendship. Appreciation also goes to Laurie Grossman for her thoughtfulness and caring. And to Ilya Pratt and Lori Lewis for their presence, good humor, and fantastic Chicken Maribel. Overall, the parent community at Park Day School has been embracing and supportive. I could not be more fortunate than to be a part of this special kinship.

You might not be aware that I have my own personal Cookie Monster, who keeps my family and visitors plied with sweets, especially his world-famous chocolate chip cookies. Thanks to Paul Bostwick for keeping us "in the sweet."

Throughout my journey to more than forty progressive schools, I was always welcomed by the principals, heads of school, and school leaders, who spent many hours allowing me to interview them and capture the culture and spirit of each school community. I so appreciate the red-carpet treatment that was afforded me by educators all over the country in public, charter, and independent schools. Many of their voices are quoted in this book, as they are the real practitioners bringing forward each day the lineage and vision of Progressive Education. I especially want to thank Neal Wrightson from Community Children's School for his loyalty and kindness. Closer to home, my friends and colleagues Terry Edeli, Cathy Hunter, and Steve Morris were by my side. Park Day School was in Terry's capable hands while I was on sabbatical leave; Cathy kept me warmed with soup and meals and fantastic good cheer; and Steve stepped up to serve on an important school transition committee to help us after I was diagnosed.

My heartfelt appreciation to Ayelet Waldman for her kindhearted Foreword. I've hardly touched the ground since receiving it.

As a side note to heads of schools and teachers who weren't mentioned in the book, I hope you will understand that I wish I could have visited and written about all of the terrific things you're doing to make learning joyful and keep our great traditions alive. Thank you for your devotion to progressive practices, and to your students. And I hope that you will get involved with the Progressive Education Network and reach out to other schools to help them along.

Finally, this project would not have been possible without the collaboration of my writing partner Katherine Ellison. Katherine contributed a vision for the structure and tone of the book and contributed significantly to the research. I learned so much about writing and forever owe her a debt of gratitude for helping to shape the book. She has worked under a great deal of pressure and is always a delight to work with, meeting deadlines and keeping commitments. I am so lucky to be in partnership with Katherine.

My family has been my constant inspiration, propelling my work and supporting my pilgrimage to tour progressive schools. My daughter Courtney understands how essential it is to be inclusive; my son Matt probes deeply into some of the hardest questions; and my sister Tess is always encouraging. And, literally every step along the way, I have been held, embraced, and sheltered by the love of my life, my wife and best friend, Elizabeth, who loves, nurtures, and inspires me every day. I could never endure were it not for her constant love and care.

As ironic as it may sound under the circumstances, like Lou Gehrig, I do feel like the "luckiest man on the face of the earth."

Photograph by Elizabeth Little

Katherine Ellison: Like any great school, this book benefited from the caring attention of extraordinary parents. They include: Michelle Mercer and Bruce Golden, who generously supported our partnership and so enthusiastically cheered us both on; Frances Dinkelspiel, a brilliant friend and matchmaker; Bonnie Nadell, who went beyond the call of duty to help us shape our proposal; Katy Dalgleish, who took a full week for an expert and thorough review of the manuscript; Maureen Cheever, who has supported the book from its inception, and also helped review it, ensuring its pedagogical gravitas; Amy Cherry, who so fortunately shared our vision, and Ann Adelman, whose diligence saved us from many a potential embarrassment, and Remy Cawley, who hung in with the project with expert and always cheerful tenacity. John Orbon and Cathy Shields at Park Day School have also been major friends of this book—with John even stepping in as content consultant and photographer—thank you!

I'm additionally deeply grateful to my writing group, North 24th Writers, without whom writing would be so much less joyful and inspired, not to mention the scones: Allison Bartlett, Leslie Berlin, Leslie Crawford, Frances Dinkelspiel, Sharon Epel, Susan Freinkel, Katherine Neilan, Lisa Okuhn, Julia Flynn Siler, and Jill Storey. I'm also indebted to Nan Weiner, for her skillful editing advice, and of course, as always, to my dear husband, Jack Epstein. Thanks, too, to the many teachers, students, parents, and experts interviewed in this book, who took time from their busy lives to help us capture the daily magic that goes on in progressive schools.

Finally, I'm most grateful of all to Tom Little, for graciously sharing with me a dream that was exclusively his for so many years. I quickly understood why he is so deeply and widely beloved. He has changed many lives, including mine, for the better. I hope that the book he has dreamed of for so long will serve to extend his compassionate influence in the world.

Index

Page numbers beginning with 219 refer to endnotes.
Page numbers in *italics* refer to illustrations.